MW01625459

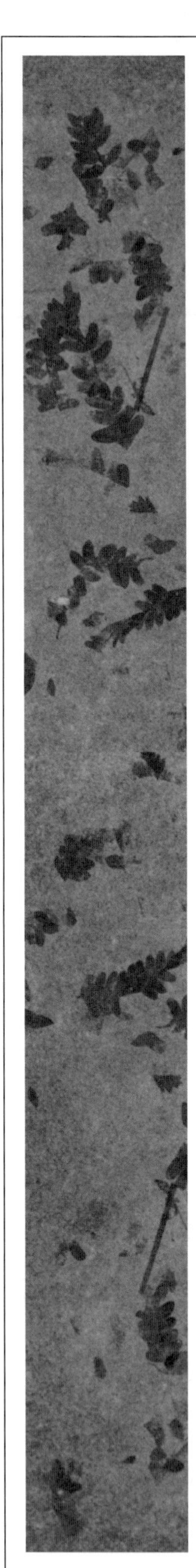

Complete text for cover artwork
Calvin
can be found on pages 134 – 135.

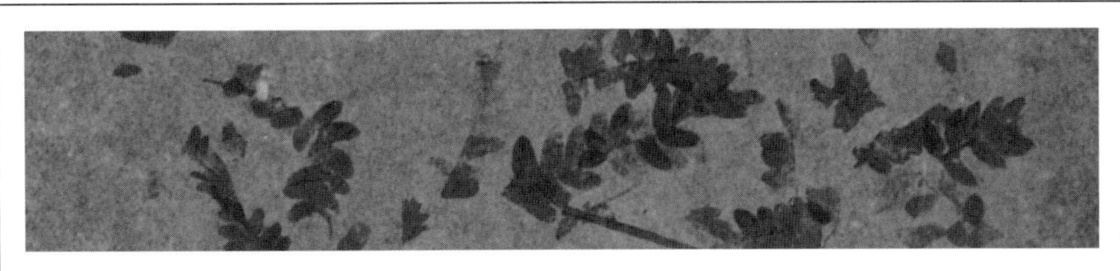

Teaching Hand Papermaking

A Classroom Guide

Gloria Zmolek Smith

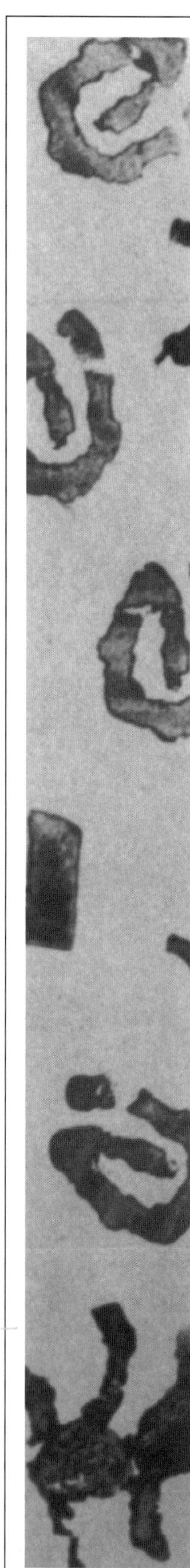

Teaching Hand Papermaking: A Classroom Guide
was edited and designed by
Jensen Management/Communications
1611 Pinehurst Drive NE, Suite 8A
Cedar Rapids, Iowa 52402–5847
Project Editor Jill J. Jensen

Cover artwork:
Calvin © 1989 by Gloria Zmolek Smith, with text by Laurel Kirstein Smith
Complete text for *Calvin* is found on pages 134 – 135.

Library of Congress Catalog Card Number 94–93961
ISBN 0–9644582–0–9

The artwork on the cover and examples of handmade paper used as
design elements throughout the text were made by Gloria Zmolek Smith.

Library of Congress Cataloging-in-Publication Data

Smith, Gloria Zmolek.
Teaching hand papermaking : a classroom guide / Gloria Zmolek Smith ; with a question and answer section on the Science of papermaking by Timothy Barrett.
p. cm.
ISBN 0964458209

1. Paper, Handmade—Study and teaching. 2. Decorative paper—Study and teaching. 3. Art—Study and teaching.

TT870 745.54 94–93961
CIP

First Edition

Published by
Zpaperpress
384 – 21st Street SE, P.O. Box 1294, Cedar Rapids, Iowa 52406–1294
319 / 365 – 9611

Printed in the United States of America

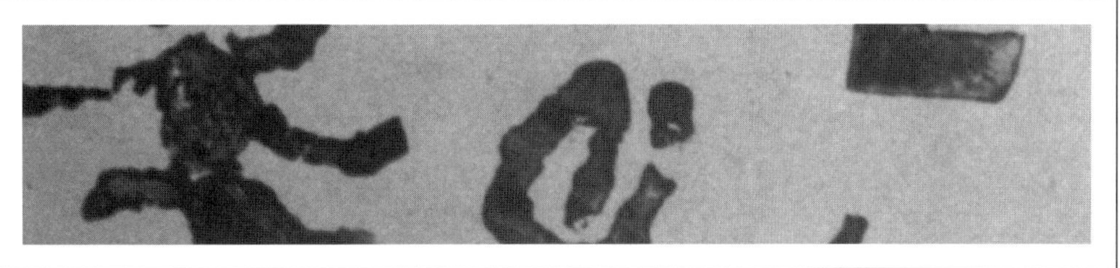

Teaching Hand Papermaking

A Classroom Guide

Gloria Zmolek Smith

with a question and answer section on
the Science of Papermaking
by *Timothy Barrett*

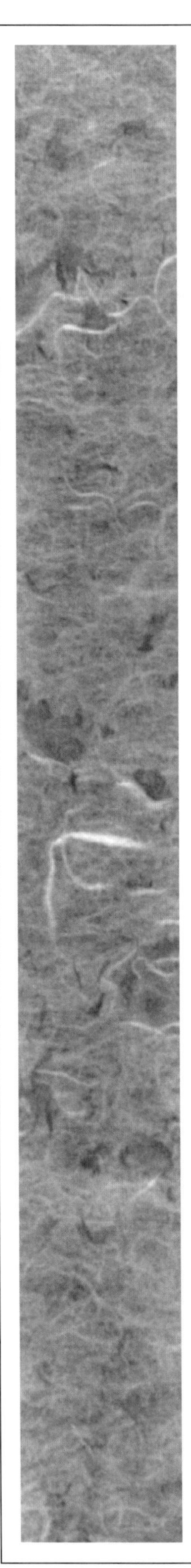

DEDICATION

To the memory of Dard Hunter

a remarkable artist, craftsman, paper historian, world traveler, and author of numerous books on papermaking, including *Papermaking in the Classroom*, published in 1931.

Dard Hunter's sons, Dard , Jr., age 14, and Cornell, age 12, posing for a photograph for their father's book Papermaking in the Classroom

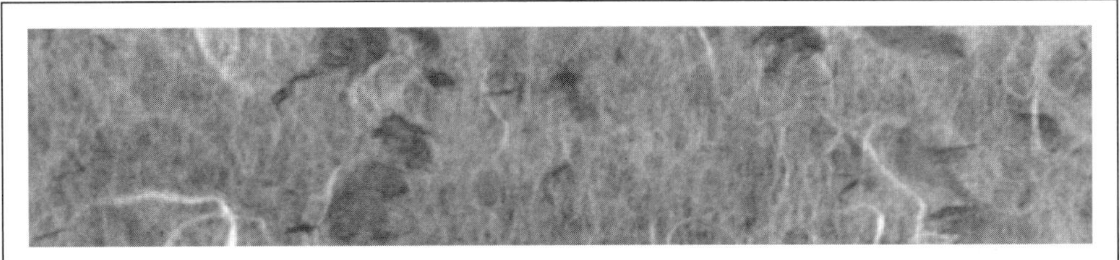

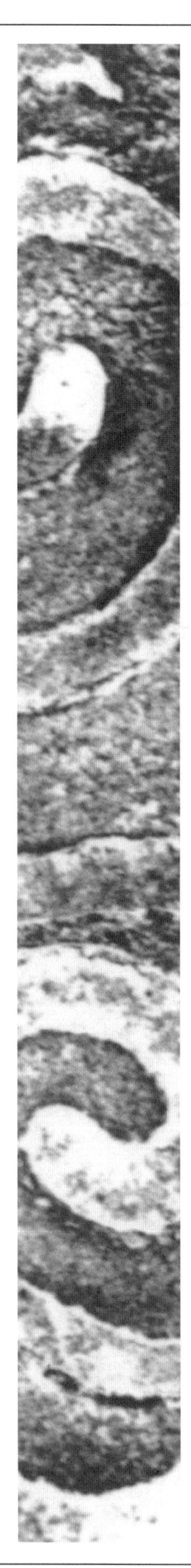

ACKNOWLEDGEMENTS

More than anyone else, I wish to thank Jill Jensen, my editor, my photographer, my designer, and my friend. She has worked tirelessly to help me write and publish this book without any guarantee of monetary reward. Without her encouragement, I doubt I would have completed the book.

I also want to thank my family: Tom, for believing in what I am doing and for his willingness to take the financial risk of self-publishing; Nathan and Laurel, for the art work that I asked them to provide, and for being self-sufficient and helpful during times when I was writing. I thank my parents, Bill and Jean, who taught me perseverance, and both my parents and my parents-in-law, Daphne and Lloyd, who have been helpful in caring for my children at various times, enabling me to pursue my career.

I thank the excellent papermakers with whom I have had the opportunity to study — Tim Barrett, Karen Stahlecker, Don Farnsworth and Neal Bonham, and all of the many papermakers I have met who have so openly shared their knowledge with me. I thank the following people who read my manuscript and offered valuable criticism, suggestions and encouragement: Neal Bonham, Suzanne Ferris, Tim Barrett, Mina Takahashi, Nancy Carey, Pam Purnell, Helen Hiebert, Gertrude Simon and Lee Scott McDonald.

I thank the Iowa Arts Council, the Ambroz Arts Advisory Board, and the many PTAs and schools which have provided funding for my residencies, enabling me to develop my ideas, which I present in this book.

I thank all my family and friends who offered encouragement along the way.

Finally, I thank Lucy Wallingford for giving me the idea that it was possible to teach papermaking in the classroom setting; Bobbie Lippman, whose survey convinced me of the need for this book; and all of the hundreds of children who have encouraged me by their wide eyes, "oohs" and "aahs," smiles, hugs and delight.

Gloria Zmolek Smith
December 1994

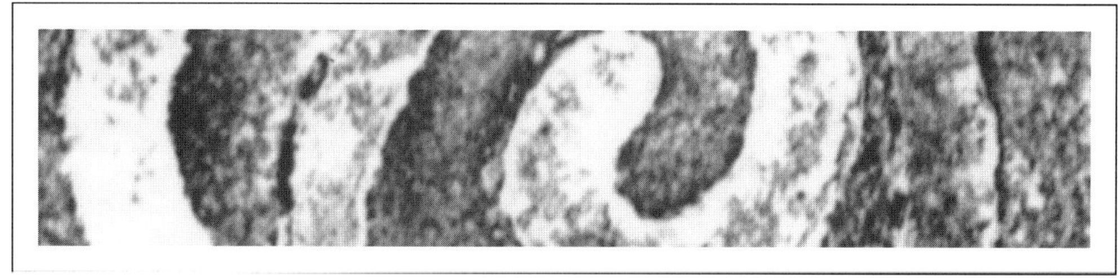

Teaching Hand Papermaking

A Classroom Guide

Gloria Zmolek Smith

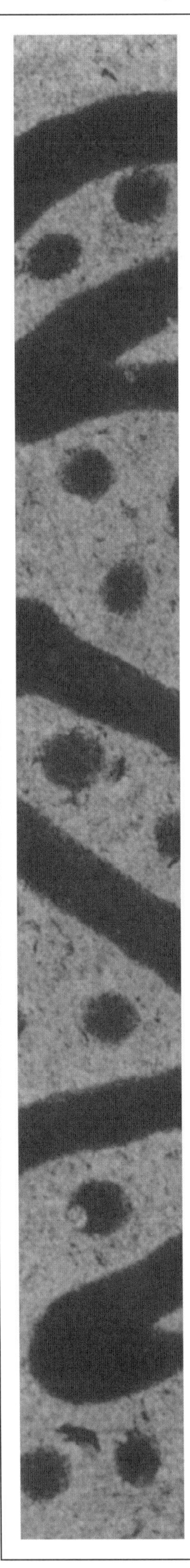

Contents

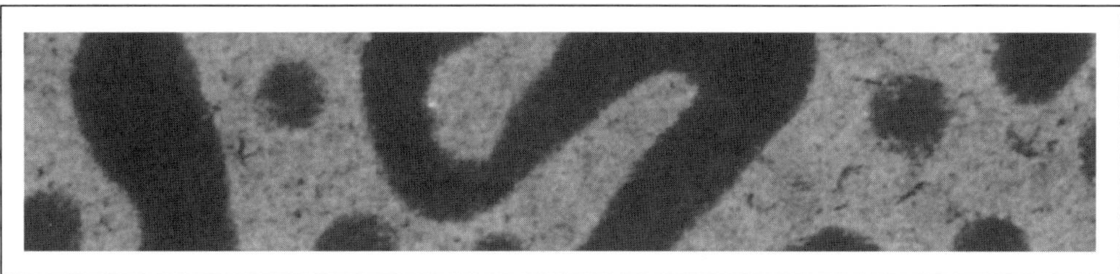

Seven • INTEGRATING PAPERMAKING with BASIC CURRICULA

ANNOTATED BIBLIOGRAPHY

APPENDIX

Reproducible Handouts

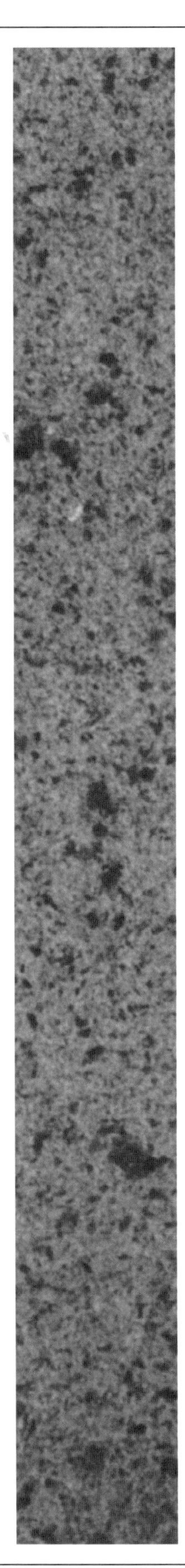

Preface

Having taught art in public school systems for five years, I asked myself, after learning how to make paper: "Could I teach 24 children (or more) how to make paper in 40 minutes (or less)?" My immediate response was "No way." But a couple years down the road, at a meeting of the Friends of Dard Hunter in Reno, Nevada, when I attended the workshop on teaching papermaking to children by a woman named Lucy Wallingford, I began to feel that it just might be a possibility.

I returned home and applied to the Iowa Arts Council for acceptance to their roster, teaching 1– to 4–week papermaking residencies for schools and communities.

It's now five years and many papermaking residencies later. My own techniques for working in the classroom are more developed and, in this book, I'll share them with you.

There are two basic hand papermaking techniques, Western and Eastern (Japanese). This book focuses on Western papermaking. I'll briefly tell you how to make paper, but that's not my primary purpose here. The purpose of my book is two–fold. One is to offer suggestions on how it's possible to teach papermaking in a standard K-12 school-

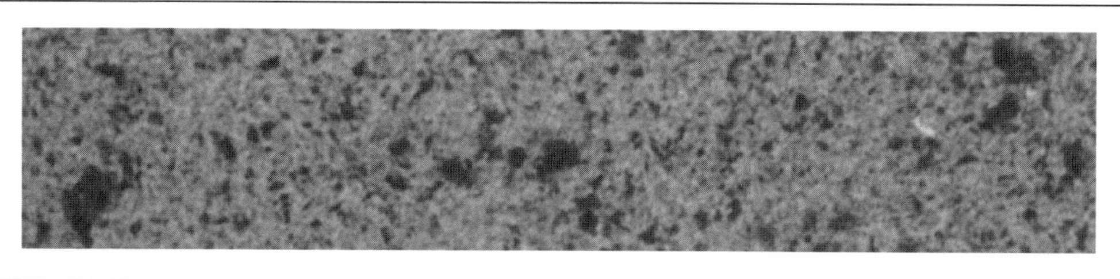

room setting. The second part of my purpose is to provide ideas for integrating hand papermaking with the basic curricula, as well as with the art curricula. If you've never made paper before, I encourage you to take a class or a workshop. You can also refer to some of the excellent resources listed in my bibliography for more information.

In addition to outlining equipment you will need, methods for managing a classroom of papermakers and some of the many techniques you can use to create art with pulp as a medium, I have developed auxilliary curriculum suggestions to help you integrate papermaking with the basic disciplines of science, math, social studies and language arts. Curriculum suggestions for integrating papermaking with the visual art disciplines, such as photography, computer graphics, sculpture, painting and drawing, are also provided.

Papermaking can be done quite simply and easily, but the possibilities of the medium are endless. If you are like me (Gloria in Paperland), one thing will lead to another, and in no time, you'll find yourself wondering how you got so involved and how papermaking became so complex. However, the joy and wonder and excitement of the children is worth all the extra effort you put forth.

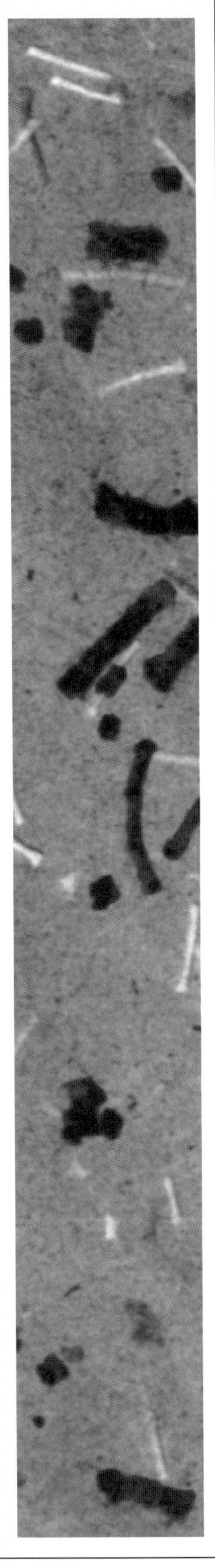

Chapter One

Tools

Tools for papermaking range from equipment that costs thousands of dollars to equipment you scrounge from your basement, garage, and kitchen.

My first adventures with papermaking were launched using a blender, an old picture frame with window screening stretched across it, a dishpan, and an old bedsheet ripped up into rectangles. As I can afford it, I purchase or make more sophisticated tools. However, I still keep my simple, inexpensive tools and I always teach my students how to make and use them. I feel it is important for students to be able to continue making paper on their own; this makes it possible for their classroom experience to become a part of their lives.

If you can afford to buy tools, that's wonderful. But if your budget is very tight, you can still make paper, using tools that can be made with very little expense. The following chapter discusses both tools you can purchase and tools you can make. I'm sure there are even more possibilities than what I suggest here, so I'll encourage you to try your ideas.

If you are not familiar with the papermaking process, you can read in this book about "Pulp" in Chapter Two and "Sheetforming" in Chapter Three, or refer to books on papermaking listed in the Bibliography, to put into perspective the following discussion of *Tools*.

MOULDS AND DECKLES

A mould (also spelled *mold*) is a screen-covered frame on which paper is formed. The deckle is an open frame placed atop the mould, which defines the edges of the sheet of paper by keeping the pulp on the screen.

I recommend using no more than eight (8) moulds for a class. Since an average class size is usually about 24 students, that gives approximately a 1-to-3 mould-to-students ratio. With too many moulds, clean-up time is increased and too many children may have too many problems at one time. When students work in groups, they learn from each other and learn to share.

PURCHASED MOULD AND DECKLE

You can purchase moulds and deckles from a papermaking supplier. (See page 156.) For many reasons, I recommend using a small mould (5-1/2"x8-1/2") for an average size class. The bigger the mould, the bigger sheets of paper you can make, but all other pieces of papermaking equipment must then be larger, too — and everything takes up more classroom space. When making larger sheets, pulp vats must be larger, your stack dryer has to be larger, and drying time for a sheet of paper increases.

Purchased moulds and deckles offer a twofold advantage. Purchasing saves construction time, and the moulds and deckles are probably going to be sturdier and hold up better over a longer period of time than ones you might make. Purchased moulds are covered with a heat-shrinking polypropylene screening which remains taut far better than window screening material. The disadvantage is, of course, the expense. Often, your decision will be guided by the size of your budget and by the amount of use your moulds will receive. However, purchased moulds are one of the first expenses I recommend you afford.

FOUND MOULDS

Picture Frame Mould • One of the cheapest and easiest types of mould to construct can be made from an old wooden picture frame (or any type of existing frame), by stretching fiberglass window screen, mosquito netting, or similar materials across it and stapling around the edges. Parents could be asked to donate their unused household frames. The simpler the frame, the better.

Typical purchased mould

You may encounter various problems with donated frames: finding enough frames of uniform size so they can all fit in the same size vat; corner joints becoming loose; screening becoming slack and needing to be restretched. (A heat shrinking polypropylene screen can be ordered from suppliers and will remain taut, solving the restretching problem.) However, if your budget is tight and you will use the moulds for only occasional classes, this can be a good solution.

Picture frame moulds can be used either without a deckle, or with a matching frame used for the deckle. When forming a sheet on a mould without a deckle, pulp may run off the edges, resulting in a thinner and possibly weaker sheet of paper. You can compensate for that somewhat by adding more pulp to the vat.

Duct Tape/Aluminum Screen Mould • This type of mould is very simple, inexpensive, and easy to make. You are limited to smaller sizes — not larger than six inches by six inches (6" x 6"), since the screen is not rigidly supported.

Cut the aluminum screen to the desired size. Cover the outside edges of the screen with duct tape. (I use a tape which I mail order from Lee Scott McDonald that is more waterproof than duct tape and, therefore, holds up longer.) The taped edges provide surfaces for holding and for protecting hands from being scratched by the edges of the screen. Although with screen moulds, you are only able to make a small piece of paper at a time, bigger pieces can be created by overlapping two or more small pieces. I use screen moulds with smaller children to teach them the concept of overlapping. No deckle is used with a duct tape/aluminum screen mould.

L to R: Duct tape/aluminum screen mould, needlepoint canvas mould, duct tape/ needlepoint canvas mould

Needlepoint Canvas Mould • A needlepoint canvas square can be used like the duct tape/aluminum screen moulds described earlier. You can use canvas without duct tape because canvas doesn't scratch. However, you can also use it with duct tape to provide a place for hands to grasp and a way to avoid thumb holes or marks in the piece of paper. Because the canvas is coarse, such a screen does not work with finely beaten pulp. No deckle is used with this mould.

Embroidery Hoop Mould • Fiberglass window screening stretched across an embroidery hoop is a great mould for making circular paper. This mould can be used either without a deckle or with another embroidery hoop as a deckle.

Deckle Box Mould • I do not use a deckle box, but I know of several classroom instructors who do. If you want to learn more, detailed instructions for making one can be found in Arnold Grummer's book *Paper by Kids*.

Stretcher Bar Mould • Begin with 8 stretcher bars. You can use bars made for stretching canvas for paintings, available in art supply stores, or you can use smaller needlepoint stretcher bars, found in sewing and crafts stores. Remember that the size of the finished paper will be the *inside* dimensions of the frame. For example, with eight stretcher bars that are 8 inches long and 3/4-inch wide, the finished size of your paper is 6-1/2" x 6-1/2".

Assemble the stretcher bars to form two frames. After checking that each frame is square, you'll need 16 screws (eight for each frame) to reinforce all corner joints. Screw two 1/2-inch to 3/4-inch brass screws on either side of the miter at each corner. (For needle-point stretcher bars, use 8 screws, one in each corner.)

Next, while not absolutely necessary, it's a good idea to polyurethane your moulds and deckles to make them more water resistant, help them last longer and help them stand up better to the use and abuse they will receive in the classroom.

To complete the mould, stretch window screening across one of the frames and use stainless steel staples to secure the screening to the edge of the frame. For a longer-lasting screen, heat-shrinking polypropylene screening can be purchased from papermaking suppliers to use on the mould. To attach the screen to the mould, follow the instructions that the supplier sends along with the screening.

To finish the deckle, attach self-adhesive foam insulating strips to each edge of the bottom side of the frame to be used as the deckle. Adding the foam helps create a tight fit between the deckle and mould.

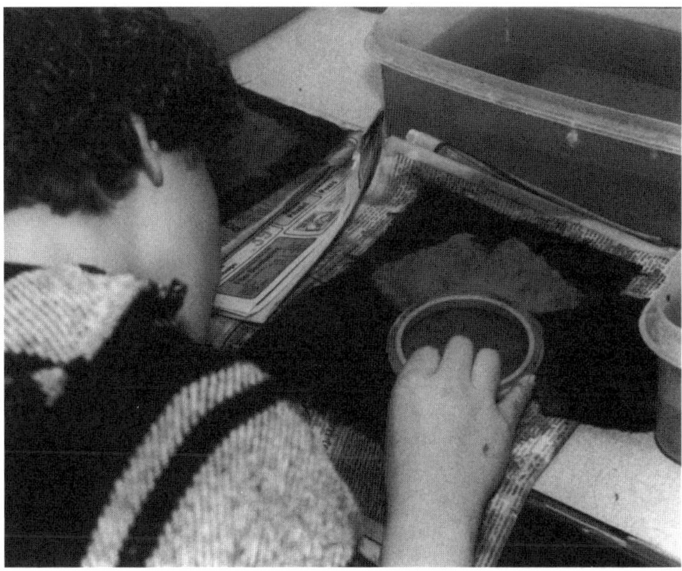

"Overlapping" papers, using an embroidery hoop mould

Stretcher bar mould using "painters'" bars

Papermaker couching a sheet, using traditional ribbed mould

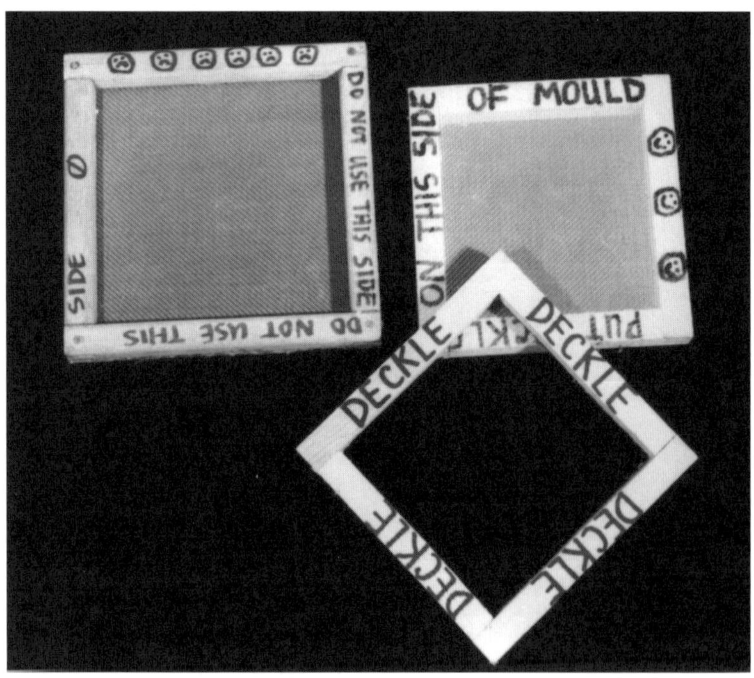

Clearly labeled moulds and deckles are helpful for beginning papermakers

LABELING MOULDS AND DECKLES

Traditional moulds have ribs on the back, making it easy to distinguish between the top of the mould (where the paper is formed) and the bottom of the mould. However, with the simpler "ribless" moulds outlined in this chapter, beginning papermakers commonly make the mistake of trying to form the sheet on the bottom of the mould. For this reason, I label the moulds and deckles. Labeling reinforces the new vocabulary words that you hope students will learn, and results in fewer mistakes. On the deckle, I write "deckle." On the top of the mould, I write "mould" and "Put deckle on this side of mould." For non-readers, you can use a symbol, such as a smiley face. On the back of the mould, I write "Do not use this side," and for non-readers, I use another symbol, such as a "frowny" face.

VATS

Vats are containers used to hold water and pulp. The vat must be larger than the size of your mould and deckle.

For classroom use, Rubbermaid™ rectangular 2.2 gallon Servin' Savers™ are great, since they are slightly larger than the 5-1/2"x 8-1/2" moulds I use and they come with watertight, sealable lids. They allow me to carry pulp to and from schools, and because they are small, students can handle them and help me load and unload. The containers are helpful when the room where I am teaching is also used for other activities. When tables must be quickly cleared off at the end of a class, these containers can have the lids snapped on and be stacked in a corner in a matter of minutes.

For larger moulds, an inexpensive solution is to use plastic cement-mixing tubs, available at building materials or lumber supply stores.

Litter boxes, dish pans, and old baby bathtubs are just a few examples of usable "found" pulp vats. The minimum depth that I recommend for a vat is approximately 5 inches. Generally, with larger moulds, greater depth is needed to achieve adequate pulp coverage of the mould.

Easy-to-make vat, using boards and plastic sheeting

If you need a particular size, you can make a simple vat from four boards and plastic sheeting. The width of the board defines the depth of the vat. The length of the board defines the size of the perimeter of the vat.

Connect the four boards at the corners to form the sides of a box, open at both the top and bottom. Place the box frame on a solid surface. Drape a sheet of plastic across the frame, letting the plastic settle inside the box until it meets the bottom surface. Use string or elastic cords to tie the excess plastic on the outside of the box, and you have an instant vat!

Hollander beater

BEATERS

Hollander Beater • Papermakers use Hollander beaters to beat pulp. By varying the beating time, you can change the quality of the pulp and, therefore, the quality of the paper.

Wooden paddles can be used singly or in pairs for beating fiber into pulp

For example, pulp that has been beaten for a short time generally produces paper that is soft and flexible and shrinks minimally when drying. Pulp that has been beaten for a long time (as much as four hours or longer) produces paper that is crisp and strong and shrinks a great deal.

Hollander beaters are expensive and would be prohibitively expensive for most classrooms. However, if you teach in a large school district, and a beater could be shared by all district schools for papermaking, such a purchase may be cost-effective. Hollander-beaten pulp can be ordered, beaten to your specifications, from most papermaking suppliers. If there is a papermaker in your area, you may be able to order beaten pulp from them and save yourself the expense of shipping the pulp.

Wooden Paddles, Rocks and Other Hard Objects • Originally, pulp was beaten by placing raw fiber on a flat surface and pounding continually until it came apart. Demonstrating or using this technique is a good way for students to develop a useful understanding of the papermaking process and an appreciation of how machines make our lives easier. You can try this method when processing plant fibers. Although not as efficient as a blender, you can make recycled paper and sheet pulp this way, too. Sometimes, I briefly demonstrate pounding recycled paper with a wooden paddle or rock, so students can better understand what the machine is doing. Since it is rather tedious and noisy, I recommend students come in either before or after school to create pulp in this manner.

Blender • A blender is usually within most classroom budgets. I have purchased many for five dollars or less at thrift stores or garage sales. You can recycle paper with a blender and you can also process many types of sheet pulp. Plant fibers can be processed if they are cut into small enough pieces and cooked long enough before placing them in the blender. Be aware, however, that a blender cuts and chops the fiber rather than pounding and beating the fibers, as does a Hollander beater. When using a blender, you cannot vary the quality of your fiber or the quality of your paper.

Processing enough pulp to use for a classroom of students takes time, so I recommend that a small group of students be encouraged to help you with this preparation either before or after school.

CAUTION: TRYING TO PROCESS TOO MUCH PULP AT ONE TIME CAN BURN OUT THE BLENDER'S MOTOR.

Hydropulper, Whiz Mixer • While not cheap, these machines are much less expensive than a Hollander beater and can be purchased from papermaking suppliers. By performing basically the same operation as a blender, they are able to make much larger quantities in much less time.

Invent Your Own • I've known papermakers to come up with many innovations of their own for processing pulp. One papermaker told about putting sheet pulp in pillow cases before putting them in his washing machine. I've experimented with a paint mixer attached to a hand drill. If you have an idea of your own, be sure to try it.

Large quantities of pulp can be hydrated using a garbage pail and a whiz mixer

FELTS

Felt is the term used for the fabric onto which wet paper is couched (rhymes with "smooched"). To couch means to transfer the freshly made sheet of paper from the mould onto another surface. The term *couch* comes from the French word *coucher*, meaning "to lay." The function of a felt is to aid in pulling the paper off the mould and to help in removing water in the pressing. The surface of the felt imprints onto the piece of paper, making it possible to vary the surface of the paper by using felts with different textures.

Wool is the traditional material used for felts. You can still order wool felts from papermaking suppliers, although they are quite costly.

A felted wool blanket, while not quite as thick as felts made specifically for papermaking, will work. Woven wool blankets may also be used, but unless the edges are finished, threads continually unravel.

Synthetic felt is another type you can order from a papermaking supplier. The synthetic felts I have used are functional, but in time, they become "hairy," making it sometimes difficult to remove delicate sheets of paper after the sheets have been pressed. Blends of synthetic and wool felts are also available.

Craft felt that can be purchased at a fabric store is another alternative. Craft felt is usually thinner than felts purchased from a papermaking supplier. It is usually made of a synthetic material.

My first felts were old cut up bedsheets. At the time, I didn't have a "real" paper press, so I pressed moisture out of the paper with a sponge. Then, I hung the section of bedsheet with the paper attached on a clothesline to dry. The bedsheet helped restrain the paper when drying, so it came out fairly flat. When dry, I simply peeled the paper from the bedsheet. The disadvantage of using bedsheets is that they are thin and do not absorb a lot of moisture. My results have not been great when I put a post of papers in the press with bedsheets between them. When I do press with bedsheets as felts, I usually put additional materials, like towels or newspapers, in the press to help absorb the moisture.

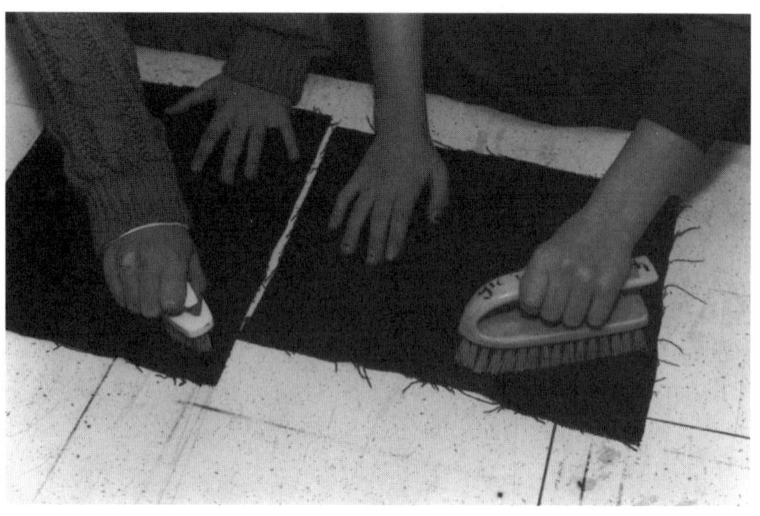

Clean felts with a scrub brush after use and hang to dry

Another material commonly used by papermakers for felts is pellon interfacing, which can be purchased from fabric stores or papermaking suppliers. I recommend buying the heaviest weight available. Like bedsheets, pellon does not absorb much moisture, but unlike bedsheets, it doesn't ravel and it dries quickly.

If you have any fabric on hand, try it. Old towels and just about any fabric you can think of will work with varying degrees of success. If you're lucky enough to have a paper mill in your area, they might give you their discarded felts, which you can cut up and use in the classroom.

Felts should be about 4 inches larger than the size of the sheet of paper you are making. For example, when making a 5-1/2"x 8-1/2" sheet of paper, felts should be approximately 9-1/2" x 12-1/2". Clean felts by laying them on a table and brushing them off with a scrub brush. Hang to dry.

PRESSES

A press is simply something that removes water from couched paper.

Purchased Press • If you have an unlimited budget, papermaking suppliers have wonderful presses you can buy! The size of the press should be determined by the size of papers you expect to press and by the space available in your facility to store the press. Obviously, larger sheets of paper require larger presses. In addition to presses, vacuum systems which can also press your paper are available.

Sponge and Fiberglass Screen/ Pellon Variations • A sponge-and-screen press is probably the most low-tech and inexpensive way to go. Just cover the wet sheet of paper with a screen or a pellon, to prevent the paper from tearing. Then, press the paper with the sponge, wringing the sponge from time to time, until you have removed as much water from the paper as possible. Placing dry newspapers underneath the felt helps absorb additional moisture. Variations on this basic method could be to place a dry felt or blotter paper on top to absorb moisture. Pressure could be applied by rolling a rolling pin over the paper surface. Use whatever works best for you.

Pressing paper in author's 20-ton hydraulic press

Low-Tech Presses • By stacking papers one on top of another, putting a board on top, and adding weight, you have a press. (In his book *Japanese Papermaking,* Timothy Barrett suggests placing a garbage pail on the top board and filling the pail with water to create pressure.) Students might want to stand on the top board to add weight, but I would discourage this practice, especially in a classroom setting, because students may be careless and slide off the stack, injuring themselves.

Sponge and fiberglass press

Found Presses • For several years, I used a bookbinder's press (a screw-type press) that had been given to me. While it was wonderful for pressing papers, because I travel to teach, the weight of this press was a drawback. However, if someone offers you a bookbinder's press, grab it! Just be sure that on the occasions you need to move it, you find able-bodied souls to help. Although I've only tried the bookbinder's press, you may find other types of presses — such as an apple cider press, which I'm sure can be adapted to your purposes. Printing presses or wringer-type presses may be used, although they are not very efficient because pressing more than one sheet at a time is difficult.

Pressing paper in author's classroom press

Paper drying on clothesline

Portable Classroom Press • The press I currently use in the classroom is similar to the one designed by Arnold Grummer. Simple instructions for making this press can be found in his book, *Paper by Kids* (see Bibliography). Grummer also sells his presses ready-made. I made mine in one afternoon, using a minimal amount of tools and woodworking skills. I followed his directions, with the exception that I made mine somewhat larger. I've used this press in the schools for several years and it functions very well.

If woodworking classes are available at your school, those instructors might be willing to "integrate" their activities with the art curriculum and build a press for you. You can also find instructions for building a press similar to Grummer's in Ralf Weidenmüller's book *Papermaking: The Art and Craft of Handmade Paper*. To keep the water from spilling onto the table and floor while pressing the paper, I place the press on top of several boards inside a plastic utility tub.

DRYERS

Clothesline • One simple way to dry paper is to leave it on the felt and hang everything on a clothesline. This method works best when the papers have been pressed by hand. If the paper is pressed by machine, use a minimal amount of pressure or it might be too dry to cling to the felt. The sheet might pull away from the felt and warp before it's completely dry. After the paper is dry, peel it away from the felt. When using a bedsheet as a felt, I run my fingernails across its back to start the releasing process.

Iron • In my introduction to papermaking, I was taught to dry paper by sandwiching the wet sheet of paper between two cotton cloths before pressing it on both sides with an iron until the paper was dry. Ironing results in a certain amount of warping because the sheet does not dry evenly. The advantage of using an iron is that it dries the paper quickly. After using this technique in the classroom, however, I do not recommend it. The possibility of students burning themselves is just too great. However, if you use this method, I recommend you have an adult stationed at each iron to supervise.

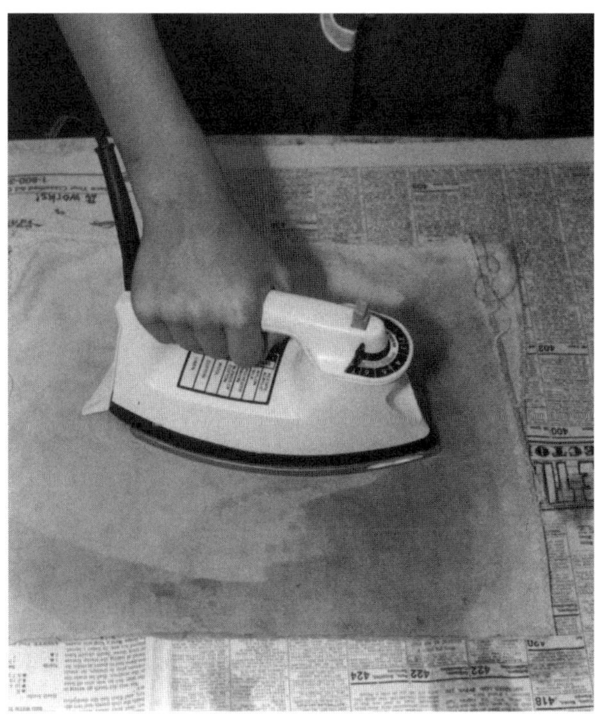

Use adult supervision when drying paper with household iron

Board and Brush • In Eastern papermaking, sheets of paper are traditionally dried by brushing them onto a board, allowing them to air-dry and peeling them off after all the moisture is removed. Paper must be pressed sufficiently to gather the strength it needs to withstand brushing, while remaining damp enough to stick to the board. You can adapt this technique by placing damp, pressed sheets of paper on windows. If the paper is strong enough, use a brush to smooth the sheets onto the glass. (Abaca, for example, has relatively long fibers and is well-suited to this technique. For shorter-fibered papers, you may have more success by patting it onto the glass with your hand.) You can also attach the sheet to any smooth surface and roll

Brush paper onto window or board to dry

across the wet paper with a rubber printing brayer. All of the paper must contact the window surface or parts may pull away and warp. Warped sheets can sometimes be flattened overnight under a stack of thick, heavy books.

Stack Dryer • Dryers may be purchased from papermaking suppliers, but I use a very simple one — corrugated cardboard (either tri-wall or bi-wall), blotter paper, and a box fan. If your budget is especially tight, make your own tri-wall cardboard by cutting up boxes and taping the pieces of cardboard together. (Perhaps a business in your town would be willing to donate cardboard.) Remember, holes in corrugated cardboard run only one direction. To insure proper air flow, all pieces of cardboard must be stacked with the holes facing the same direction.

Economical and easy–to–use stack dryer

Cut the cardboard and blotter paper to dimensions determined by the size of paper you usually make. Cut the cardboard just slightly larger than the blotter paper. I use 12" x 13" cardboard and blotter paper, so two 5-1/2" x 8-1/2" sheets fit on each layer. The stacked cardboard fits into plastic crates I carry from my studio to the schools, and the crates are small enough for children to lift. Three rows of this size cardboard fit neatly in front of two standard box fans.

Start the stack by laying a piece of cardboard on a table. Next, use one blotter sheet, followed by two side-by-side sheets of wet paper. Top this with another blotter sheet, another piece of cardboard (holes running the same direction as the first), one blotter sheet, wet papers, one blotter sheet, and so forth. Follow this sequence until you have all sheets of wet paper between blotter sheets.

Carefully place all stacks in front of the box fans, with some weight on each stack to keep top sheets from buckling. Turn on the fan. Depending on the size and thickness of the paper and stacks, as well as the amount of humidity in the air, a fan set at low speed will probably dry the paper in eight to ten hours. Faster fan speeds shorten drying times.

For more efficiency, plastic sheeting can be taped to the fan and extended over and down the sides of the stack to direct airflow.

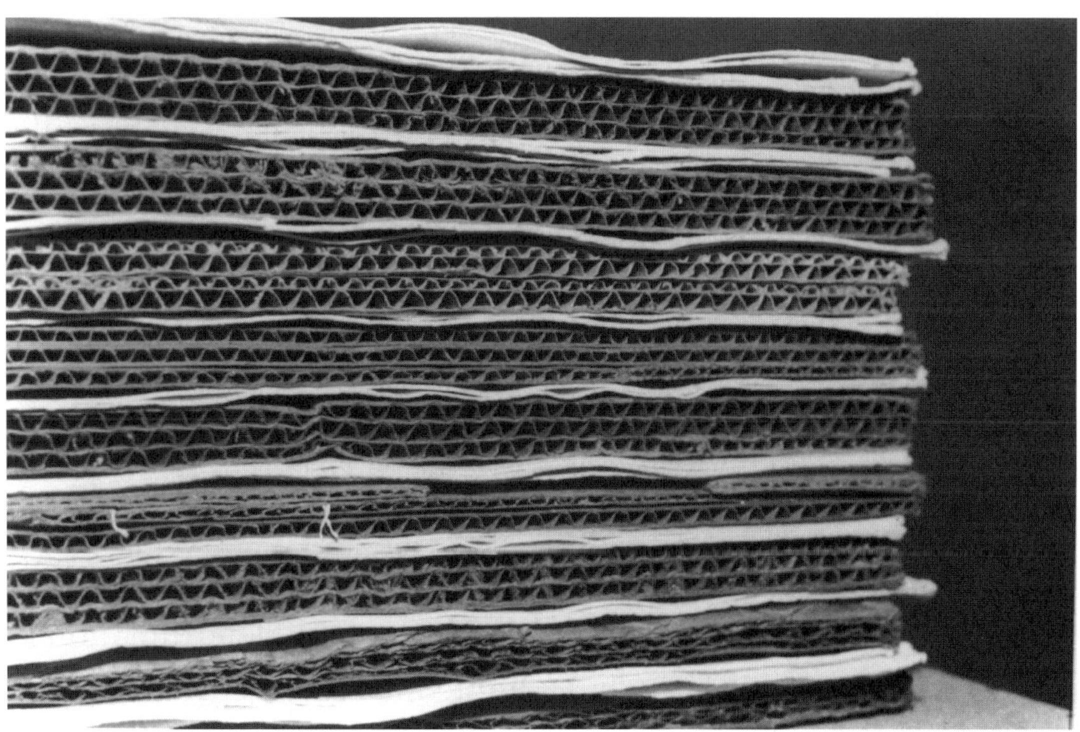

For proper airflow, all cardboard holes must face same direction

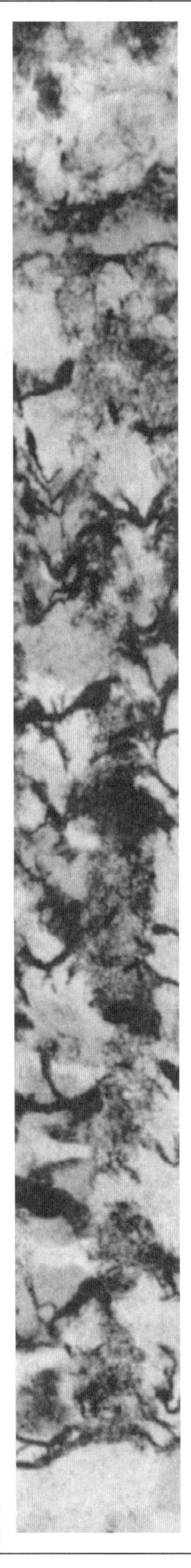

Chapter Two

Materials

Materials, like tools, can be purchased or scrounged. I clearly remember the enormous garbage bag filled with shredded medical records my husband brought home from his hospital job for me to recycle. Those shreds of other people's lives became my first paper.

After making reams of recycled paper, my next phase of papermaking involved processing all the plants in my yard and from the Iowa countryside. Iris, yucca, corn, pampas grass, cattails, and even asparagus were plant fibers that I processed into paper. Preparing them in a blender wasn't easy, but my determination prevailed. I even attempted to recycle my children's "no–longer–used" cloth diapers. While I couldn't get the diapers completely broken down, I was able to get enough of the pieces small enough to make a sheet of paper.

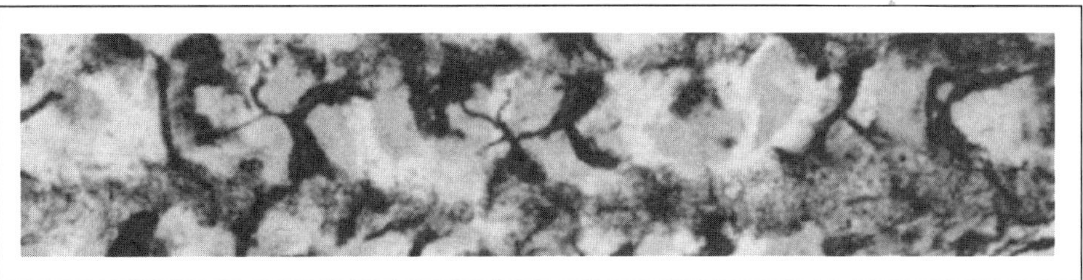

When I reached the point where the paper I could make with a blender no longer suited my needs, I learned Japanese paper-making and found that very fine paper can be made using a wooden paddle as a beater. Soon, I purchased my first exotic fiber, kozo, from Thailand. Eventually, I was able to buy a Hollander beater and begin making an incredible range of paper types.

When I teach in schools, I provide beaten pulp, usually a combination of cotton linter and abaca. I also teach children how to recycle paper. I like them to experience the range of qualities possible in handmade paper.

PULP: SOURCES and PREPARATION

Sheet Pulp • Sheet pulps are a form of dry paper pulp made from various plant fibers such as cotton linter, abaca, and flax. You can even get blue jeans pulp in sheet form. The plant fibers have been cooked and partially beaten. The pulp comes in large sheets (approximately 25 inches x 32 inches) of varying thicknesses and weight.

Many suppliers listed in the Appendix sell sheet pulps. Since some sheet pulps process well in a blender and others do not, suppliers will be happy to recommend the kind of fiber to best fit your needs. Specify the kind of paper you wish to create and let them know that you will be processing it in a blender. If you tell your suppliers how much paper you plan to make, they can recommend the approximate amount of sheet pulp you'll need.

Tools Needed to Prepare Sheet Pulp:

Bucket or other container
Blender
Sheet pulp

Processing the pulp is quite simple. Soak the sheet pulp overnight, tear it into small pieces, and process it in a blender, as you do in Step Four of Pulp Preparation, listed on page 22 under "recycled pulp." The advantage of using sheet pulps is the convenience (they can be stored indefinitely), the relatively low cost, the variety of different fibers available, and the ability to make paper of higher quality than what you will be able to make by recycling. If your budget is really tight, you might consider mixing sheet pulp with recycled pulp, to improve the quality of the paper while keeping your cost down.

Prepared Pulp • Ready–to–use beaten pulp may also be purchased from many suppliers. Be aware that the length of beating time greatly affects the type and quality of the finished paper. Pulp beaten for one hour makes a paper that is very different from paper made from pulp that has been beaten for four hours. The longer a fiber is beaten, the stronger and crisper the paper will be. Long–beaten pulp also drains more slowly and shrinks more when it dries. If you have a specific purpose for the paper, or if you have a specific type of paper that you want to make, talk to your suppliers and they will recommend the appropriate amount of beating time.

Advantages of having prepared/ beaten pulp are first, that you are able to control the type of paper you make and, second, it obviously cuts down on the amount of work that you must do. Disadvantages are the cost and the fact that beaten pulp has a limited shelf life. Beaten pulp can be frozen, but it must be reprocessed in a blender to return it near the original consistency.

Recycled Pulp • If you plan to use recycled pulp, prepare all pulp before beginning to form sheets. So you don't have to stay up half the night processing pulp, enlist a few students to prepare pulp during class, while others work on different assignments. Or perhaps some students might like to help with pulp preparation before or after school.

• SAFETY NOTE •

If children learn to recycle pulp, you can be quite sure many of them will want to try it at home. Since many children are not skilled in using stoves and/or blenders, be sure to emphasize that pulp preparation is an activity to be done only with ADULT SUPERVISION.

Tools:

Bucket or some sort of container
Stainless steel or enameled cooking pot
Long handled spoon
Colander lined with fiberglass window screen, cheese cloth, old sheer curtains, mosquito netting, or (my favorite) synthetic organdy
Hot pads

Heat source:

Hot plate or stove

Blender:

I've known many blenders and the Osterizer brand works best for me. I've never paid more than five dollars for one. Look for them at garage sales or thrift stores, or a parent may wish to donate a blender to the class.

Tools and supplies for recycling paper into pulp

PULP PREPARATION

1) *Gather the paper.*

When students collect their own paper to recycle, environmental awareness is raised. Two eye–opening activities can serve this purpose. Ask students to save all unneeded school papers for a week. When every scrap of paper is saved rather than thrown away, students become very aware of the incredible volume of paper we use. Another awareness activity would be for each student to bring in a week's worth of junk mail.

IMPORTANT:

When selecting paper to recycle, remember that the quality of the final paper depends on the quality of the paper with which you begin. For example, given the choice between computer paper and newsprint, computer paper is usually the better choice because it's a higher quality paper. If you want a very white pulp, select only those junk–mail envelopes which have very little printing.

For colored pulp without adding color after processing pulp, sort already–colored paper (such as construction paper) and prepare each color separately. Scraps of cotton rag mat board from framing shops make an excellent source of recycled pulp. Papermaker Bill Messer has a great idea — he peels the colored top layer off scraps of mat board and ends up with high quality paper to recycle. He eliminates the need to add color to his pulp *and* he's recycling!

Avoid shiny papers and papers that are designed for wet conditions, such as coffee filters. They are difficult to break down. Recycling a variety of paper helps students become sensitive to the many different types and qualities of paper.

To determine how much paper to gather, plan on recycling two or three sheets of paper for every sheet you want to make. Your recycled paper will likely be thicker than machine–made paper.

2) *Soak the paper.*

Put your collected paper in a bucket or some other sort of container. Cover all the paper with water and soak it overnight. On the following day, have the students tear the wet paper into one–inch squares.

3) *Cook the paper.*

This step is optional. When teaching elementary students, they should be cautioned that if they plan to make paper at home, they should do this activity only with **adult supervision**!

Many papermakers soak their paper and put it directly into the blender. I find, however, that cooking results in a better bonding of fibers.

Place the torn wet paper into a pot of boiling water. Simmer with the lid on for one hour, stirring about every fifteen minutes to keep the topmost paper from drying out. Cooking helps clean out any impurities and makes the fibers swell and fray, preparing them for bonding later.

Let the paper cool and line the colander with the material you've chosen for straining. Next, drain the water by pouring it through the lined colander. Remove the wet paper from the colander and stored it in a sealed plastic bag or container until you are ready to process it. Storing the wet pulp in the refrigerator extends its useful life. Pulp can be frozen indefinitely.

4) *Beat the paper.*

NOTE: If the children in your classes are like most of the children I have taught, they are not familiar with using a blender. Before you put them to work, be sure to give instructions on how to put the container on the base of the blender and how to turn the machine off and on.

Fill the blender container with four cups of water. Add a ball of cooked paper about the size of a golf ball. Run the blender until the paper is completely disintegrated. You now have paper pulp!

Adding pulp to blender

IMPORTANT:

Caution students about trying to process too much paper in the blender at one time. A blender can only handle small amounts of paper. *Processing too much paper at once will cause the blender motor to burn out.* I speak from personal experience!

Once you have finished the beating, you may want to strain the pulp to get rid of some of the water and make storage a bit easier. Again at this point, if you can, refrigerate the pulp. If you have a good relationship with your school's cafeteria personnel, they might not object to storing your pulp in their refrigerators, but be sure your containers are clearly labeled!

Unrefrigerated pulp should last at least a week, depending on the amount of warmth in your classroom. The distinctive odor tells you when the pulp is going bad! Sometimes, the life of the pulp can be extended by rinsing it very thoroughly.

Refrigerated pulp lasts quite a while longer, although the final paper quality is not as good when the pulp is more than a week old. Pulp can be drained and frozen, but to make it usable again, it must be thawed and reprocessed in the blender.

The advantages of using recycled pulp are that it costs nothing, and that it reinforces the values of recycling and concern for our environment. The disadvantages are the amount of time it takes to prepare, especially when using a blender, and the fact that the finished paper will not be as strong as paper produced directly from plant fibers.

Use proper safety precautions when adding pigment to pulp

One technique for adding strength, when necessary, to your paper is to pull and couch a sheet, cover it with a layer of cheesecloth, form *another* sheet and laminate the second sheet on top of the first one.

Another possibility for making your recycled paper stronger is to combine it with beaten pulp or with sheet pulp prepared in a blender.

COLOR

Except when recycling previously colored paper (colored construction paper, for example), color is added to pulp after beating and before sheets are formed.

• SAFETY NOTE •

Retailers of any toxic or hazardous material must have Materials Safety Data Sheets (MSDS) available for each substance they sell. These sheets tell about the materials and their health hazards. Reading the MSDS can help you avoid dangerous materials and avoid fear of safe ones.

Pigments • Professional water–dispersed pigments, the most light–fast colors a papermaker can use, are my choice for coloring paper. You may purchase them from papermaking suppliers. Although I use these professional pigments in the classroom, they are highly toxic, so I do not allow young students to color the pulp with them. However, I find advanced high school art students are able to do their own coloring. Be sure to wear rubber gloves when pigmenting pulp.

The pulp and the pigments have the same charge, so they repel each other. Adding a substance called a retention aid, which has the opposite charge, allows the pulp and pigments to come together. When properly pigmented, the pulp will be colored and the water in which the pulp floats will be clear. If the water is not clear, you may have added too little retention aid or too much pigment.

Each supplier will send you instructions for how to pigment pulp. Some recommend that you first dilute both the pigment and the retention aid with water. I follow this recommendation because I find it is easier to mix the additives more evenly.

Some suppliers suggest adding the retention aid and then adding the color. Others reverse that order. I usually add some pigment, followed by retention aid. Then I check to see if the color is being retained by placing a small amount of pulp on a blotter. If color spreads from the clump of pulp, I know I need to add more retention aid. If the color does not spread, the pigmenting process is complete — unless I decide I want a darker color, and then I might add more pigment. If it is important to achieve a specific color, a sample of colored pulp must be dried to see the final color.

Personally, I don't measure pigment amounts, although some suppliers' instruction sheets offer guidelines. Hard–and–fast rules are difficult to create because not all pigments seem to work the same. The principle which works best for me is "you can always add more," so I start with additives in small quantities and add them a bit at a time.

Remember that reaching a saturation point for both pigment and retention aid *is* possible. Adding more pigment than the fiber can accept means the water remains colored, no matter how much retention aid is added. At that point, you need to strain the pulp to get rid of excess pigment, or add more pulp to absorb the excess pigment. Too much retention aid can cause the pulp to clump or cause the fibers to repel the pigment. You can correct this problem by rinsing the pulp.

For more information on pigmenting pulp, read Bobbie Lippman's answer to the question: "Would you please explain the process of pigmenting pulp in terms a layperson can understand?" in *Hand Papermaking*, Volume 8, Number 1, Summer 1993. A thorough source for more technical information is Elaine Koretsky's *Color for the Hand Papermaker*.

Rubber gloves are not necessary once the pulp is properly pigmented. The pulp will be safe to touch because the pigment adheres to the pulp rather than your skin.

If you choose to use pigments, PLEASE READ AND FOLLOW THE DISTRIBUTOR'S DIRECTIONS for their use.

Dyes • Dyes, including RIT dye, may be used to color pulp. Because dyes are not as light–fast as pigments and because of their toxicity, I prefer not to use them. If you use dyes, please be aware of the precautions you should take when using them.

Water–Soluble Colors • For classroom papermaking, you can use just about any type of water–soluble color for your pulp, some of which will work better than others. The colors will have varying degrees of permanence. If you have something on hand, give it a try and see whether you like the results. My experiments have included food coloring, kool–aid, tempera paint, water colors, acrylics, inks and airbrush colors.

When using acrylics or tempera paint to color pulp, adding retention aid improves the bonding of pigments to the fiber, resulting in stronger–colored pulp. I have not explored using retention aid with the other coloring agents mentioned above, but my hunch is that retention aid might also help those colors attach to the fibers.

SIZING

Sizing is the substance added to pulp which makes paper more waterproof. If you plan to write, draw or paint on the paper, you might need to add sizing, so the ink or paint doesn't bleed or feather. Feathering is more likely to happen when paint or ink is thin or very liquid. Ballpoint pen ink does not usually feather, even on unsized paper. Depending on the use you have for the paper, you may or may not choose to add sizing.

Sizing can be done both externally and internally. External sizing is added by dipping the paper in a bath of the sizing substance, once the sheet is formed, pressed and dried. Internal sizing is the easiest to use because sizing is added to the pulp before the sheet is formed. For that reason, I use internal sizing and recommend it for classroom papermaking.

Liquid Sizing • You may purchase an internal sizing from any papermaking supplier. Don't purchase more than you need, because liquid sizing has a limited shelf life.

Occasionally, people have mild skin irritation when using this sizing, so you might want to skip sizing altogether, or use a milder, homemade version.

Homemade Sizing • If your budget is small, various products found in the home may also be used as sizing, including unflavored gelatin, liquid laundry starch or cornstarch. The following recipe to make your own internal sizing is reprinted from *The Complete Book of Handcrafted Paper* by Marna Elyea Kern, which is no longer in print.

Ingredients:

1 packet unflavored gelatin
2 tablespoons cold water
2 tablespoons boiling water
2 tablespoons cornstarch
1 cup boiling water

Directions:

Pour gelatin into heat–proof bowl or small saucepan.

Add 2 tablespoons of cold water and stir until the gelatin forms paste.

Add 2 tablespoons of boiling water, stirring until the gelatin is dissolved.

Stir in the cornstarch until it is also dissolved.

Then add 1 cup boiling water, mixing well. Be sure all lumps are dissolved.

When sizing paper, add approximately 1/8 teaspoon of sizing per blender of pulp.

OTHER ADDITIVES

Pigment and retention aids are the most often–used papermaking additives, and sizing will be useful to many of you, too. For more advanced papermaking techniques, many more possibilities exist, and I have listed a few of them below. Please consult papermaking suppliers' catalogues and other books on papermaking for more in–depth information.

Methyl Cellulose comes in a powder form and needs to be mixed with water. By thinning and adding it to pulp, sheets with more strength can be created for use with the casting process (see Chapter Four, page 52). Methyl cellulose can also be mixed with a small amount of water to form a paste, which can then be used as an adhesive.

Soda Ash is added to water when cooking plant fibers to dissolve impurities.

Kaolin Clay can be added to pulp as a filler to create a smooth surface and to increase the opacity of paper. Clay also helps reduce the amount of shrinkage in the pulp.

Formation Aid turns water into slime. (I know it's not a very poetic term, but that's what your students will call it!) Formation aid helps separate fibers to make them more evenly distributed, and it slows down the flow or drainage of water. Formation aid comes in powdered form, along with directions for mixing it. More information about formation aid can be found on page 56.

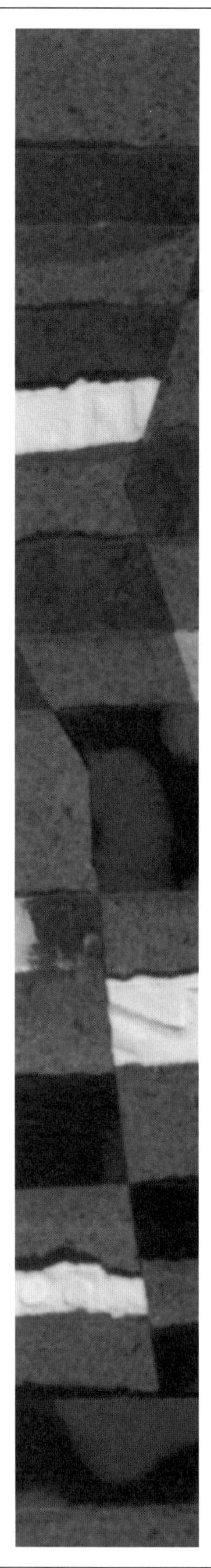

Chapter Three

Sheetforming

TECHNIQUES FOR THE CLASSROOM

Put together a group of teachers from across the country who have taught papermaking in the classroom and you'll very likely find as many different techniques as there are teachers. No single "right" way to teach papermaking exists. What I offer is a way I have found, through much trial and error, that works for me.

The first time I taught papermaking in the classroom, enough water covered the floor to classify the art room as a wading pool! I hope my ideas help you avoid such extremes. You'll certainly find, as I have, that to have papermaking work smoothly in your classroom, you are constantly prodded to innovation and adaptation. Best wishes!

DEMONSTRATION

Be sure to take your time when demonstrating the steps of papermaking. The process involves many steps and some students may have difficulty remembering all the steps with only a single demonstration. You may want to list the steps of the process on a chalkboard.

If students have not been involved in making pulp, be sure to explain how pulp is made, and briefly demonstrate using the blender to recycle paper into pulp.

If your "classroom" is on a cart which you wheel from room to room, you'll probably prefer to work with the pouring method of papermaking.

Pouring Method • The pouring method is well illustrated in the book *Paper by Kids* by Arnold Grummer (see Bibliography). You can construct or buy a deckle box, as discussed in his book, or you may use the following method for making paper.

Materials needed:

Coffee cans or similar containers
Embroidery hoops slightly larger than the circumference of the coffee can
Fiberglass window screen
Cookie cutters (open on both top and bottom)
Containers to scoop and pour pulp

Directions:

Stretch fiberglass screen across an embroidery hoop just as you would stretch fabric. Trim any excess screen.

Place the screen–covered hoop on top of the open end of the coffee can. Place a cookie cutter on top of the screen. Pour pulp inside the cookie cutter, onto the screen.

Continue pouring until the screen is covered with pulp.

Remove the cookie cutter and couch the sheet on a felt. (See section on "Felts," page 11, and information on "couching," page 35.)

Pouring Method: cookie-cutter sheetforming

For more ideas on how to use the pouring method in a classroom setting, read the article, "Cookie Cutter Papermaking" by Judith Arrowood and Catherine Brewes in the journal *Hand Papermaking*, Summer 1990, Volume 5, Number 1.

Dipping Method • In the classroom, I use the dipping method of papermaking. The ideal set–up is to have a room just for papermaking, but such facilities are not often a reality. For the dipping method, at the very least, you need space for many tables, with access to water and electricity.

CLASSROOM SET–UP

Every classroom is a little bit different. Your set–up and methods will depend on the size and space available, other activities that must share your area during the time you are making paper, and the complexity of your papermaking process.

I have tried arranging the classroom in many different ways. The arrangement that works best for me is to have tables in the middle of the room for supplies, and to surround them with student work tables. Each work table has two or three vats of pulp on it. All other equipment is kept on the supply tables. See the sample classroom diagram on the opposite page.

Each student needs a work pad of newspaper about 3 or 4 sheets thick to absorb excess water. Using this system, I have managed up to 40 children making paper without getting more than a drop or two of water on the floor. (Well, maybe, three or four!)

Plan to collect about one grocery bag of newspapers for an average class. You create fewer wet newspapers if you pull the newspapers apart, and then refold, so each layer is no more than 4 sheets thick. Then you can remove wet newspapers from the top and reuse the dry papers underneath. (Separating newspapers could be done by students in advance of the papermaking class.) If your table surface could be damaged by water, cover it first with plastic.

Because chairs generally get in the way, I put them along the walls. Then, if there is a need to restore order to the classroom, students can be directed to sit on the chairs. Occasionally, with the chairs along the walls, students have expressed uncertainty about their capability to stand up for a full 45 minutes. This gives me an opportunity to let them know what a hard life it is to be a papermaker. (I tell them I want them to have the complete experience!)

If your class time is limited, you can complete Steps 1 and 2 of the process listed below before the class arrives, so students have plenty of time to make a sheet of paper.

STEP 1 • *Fill the vat with water*

Fill the vat about half full of cold water. Using cold water extends the life of the pulp.

STEP 2 • *Add pulp to the vat*

Add approximately one–half to one cup of prepared pulp. The amount will vary depending on the concentration of your pulp mixture. The first time you add pulp, more is required than for subsequent times. Too little pulp in the vats results in sheets that are too thin. Lots of pulp results in sheets that are too thick.

One part of papermaking learned only through experience is judging the right amount of pulp for the vat. If adult volunteers are available, I have them add pulp to the vat as needed. If you are on your own, set a standard measure of pulp which each student can add to the

SAMPLE CLASSROOM SET–UP

(not to scale)

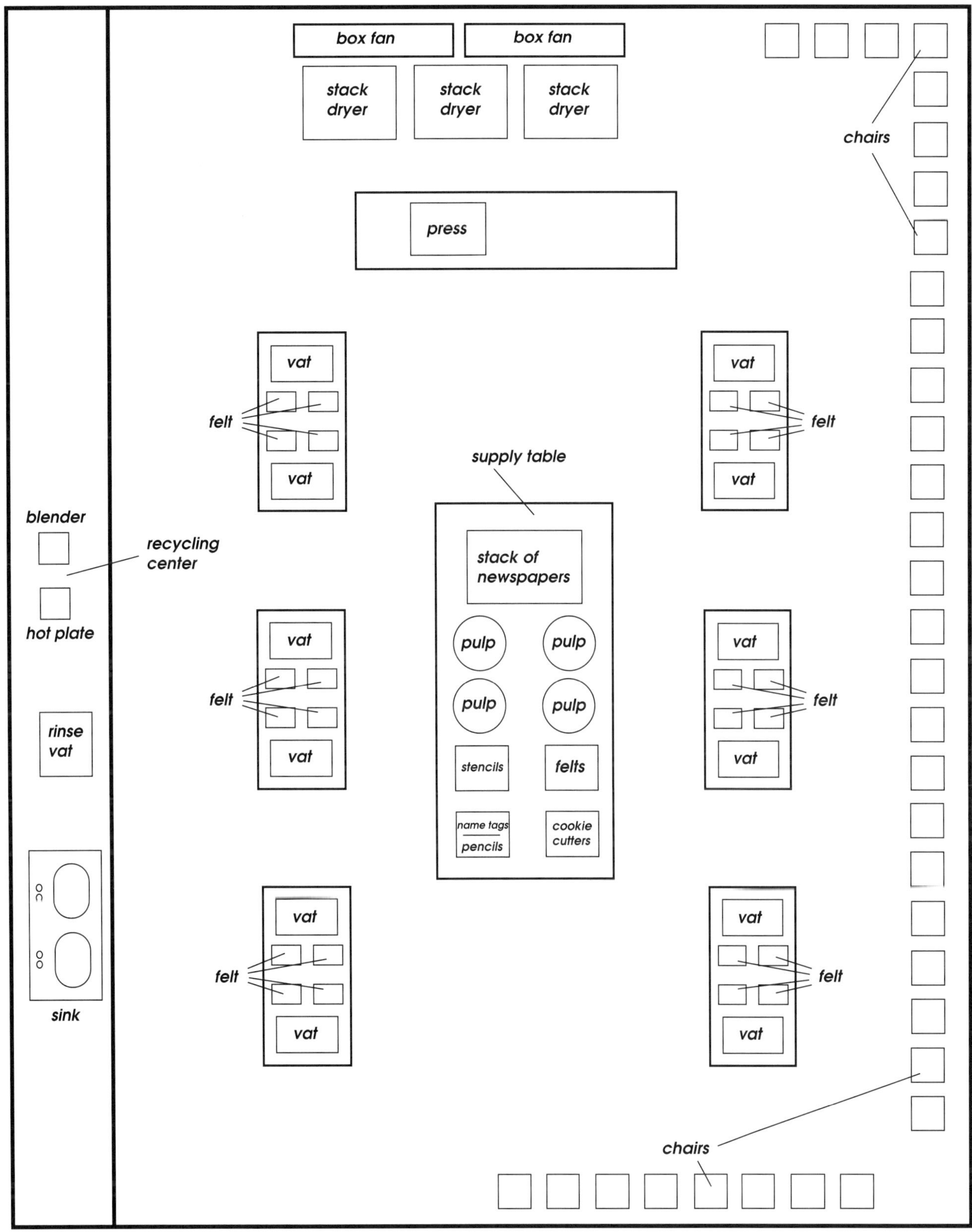

vat before forming sheets. Students are usually more interested in forming their sheets than in stirring pulp, so watering down the pulp stock helps any pulp added later to blend in better.

STEP 3 • *Prepare the felt*

Each student should put a felt on top of a stack of newspapers and place it next to the vat where they are working. For younger students, I set up stations for each student at the individual tables before they arrive. For older students, I put a stack of newspapers and a stack of felts on the supply table and they set up their own stations.

Traditionally, paper couches best on felts that are damp. However, when working with small moulds and thin felts, I find it is not always necessary to dampen felts before using them.

STEP 4 • *Stirring the pulp*

Stirring the pulp is very important in forming an even sheet. When stirring by hand, spread your fingers apart and move your hand quickly. Initially, students groan at the idea of putting their hands in the pulp, but after a short time, you will have difficulty keeping their hands out of the pulp! To avoid lots of trips to the sink to wash hands, show students that they can remove pulp from their hands by putting them in the vat and quickly pulling them out vertically.

Step 4
Stirring the pulp

STEP 5 •
Putting the mould and deckle together

Be sure students are paying attention when you put the deckle on top of the mould. Because simple moulds are made without ribs, identifying the correct side of the mould for making paper can be confusing. I often show students the mould held upside down and ask them to imagine that I have picked up pulp on the wrong side of the mould. When I turn the mould over onto the felt, I ask them why I can't couch the paper. The answer, of course, is that the pulp is not touching the felt and can't adhere to the felt because the wood of the mould creates a barrier. Labeling the mould and deckle, as described in Chapter One, is especially helpful.

Step 5 Putting the mould and deckle together

STEP 6 • *Sheetforming*

Sheetforming techniques vary from one papermaker to another. Following is my best adaptation for classroom situations of a technique for using the small vats and small moulds and deckles described in Chapter One. This technique will not work with larger moulds.

Show students how to hold the mould, by placing thumbs on the deckle and fingers on the bottom side of the mould. Be sure to demonstrate that if thumbs are put on the screen (a common classroom occurrence), pulp cannot cover those areas and thumb holes appear in the paper — fine, if thumb holes are wanted!

Hold the mould and deckle away from your body and tilt it vertically, so the top side of the

Step 6 Hold thumbs on deckle and fingers on mould, about halfway down. Hold mould vertically and "sneak" it into vat, so pulp isn't pushed around too much.

mould faces you. Submerge the mould and deckle into the vat, "sneaking" it in along the edge of the vat that is farthest away from you, so the pulp is disturbed as little as possible.

When the edge of the mould touches the bottom, slide it towards you so the entire mould lies flat, in a horizontal position at the bottom of the vat. Without hesitating, bring the mould straight up out of the vat. An ever–so–slight shake of the mould, both sideways and forward–and–back, immediately after it has been pulled to the surface of the vat will help to distribute the fibers more evenly.

Emphasize that the mould should not be tilted, or the pulp will slide to one side and form an uneven sheet of paper. Compare holding the mould horizontally to students carrying lunch trays. For younger classes, students may pantomime the technique, holding either an actual or imaginary mould, while you demonstrate.

Step 7
When bottom edge of mould hits bottom of vat, flatten entire mould so it lays on bottom of vat. Raise mould horizontally and hold over vat to drain. At this point, pulp on the mould is about 25 times thicker than the finished sheet.

Some students may not have stirred the pulp enough, which results in uneven or clumpy paper. When sheets have thin areas, it is often the result of poor sheet–pulling techniques, although students may think there is not enough pulp in the vat.

Remember that pulp is more translucent when wet, so judging if you have enough pulp on your mould may be hard. With experience, you will know how thick or thin a wet sheet will be when it is dry. For beginners, it's best to aim for sheets of medium thickness (about 3/16 of an inch). If sheets are very thin, they can tear easily and are more difficult to couch. Very thick sheets present a problem in the classroom because longer drying time is required.

STEP 7 • *Drain the mould*

Draining the mould takes only a few moments and is an important step to mention to students. Otherwise, the classroom floor can get really wet. Suggest that students count to ten while holding the mould over the vat to let the water drain. Speed up draining by tilting the mould slightly, so one corner is lower than the others.

STEP 8 • *Remove the deckle*

Set the mould down on the felt and remove the deckle. Because pulp remains on the deckle and other students need the deckle to make paper, remove the pulp with a similar method as that used for removing pulp from hands. Quickly "dash" the deckle onto the surface of the water in the vat to remove the pulp.

Step 8
Set mould down on felt and remove deckle

STEP 9 • *Couch the sheet*

When the pulp has drained enough that it will not slip from the mould, you are ready to couch the sheet. Felts are normally dampened before couching the sheet, so the paper better adheres to the felt. If your felts are not thick ones, when working small, you won't need to moisten the felt; by putting the mould on the felt and then removing the deckle, water from the mould drips on the felt and adds a bit of moisture. However, if the paper does not readily adhere to the felts, you will want to wet them.

Pick up the mould and slowly turn it over, holding the mould upside down, so students can see that once the mould is turned over, they do not have to be in a big hurry to place the sheet on the felt. Relate to students that *surface tension* (a concept learned in science) is the reason pulp clings to the mould.

Center the sheet on the felt. Once the mould is placed on the felt, press on the back of the screen with fingers or a sponge to help the paper adhere to the felt and release from the mould. Using sponges helps keep the classroom dry.

Step 9
Turn mould over and couch paper onto felt. Hold mould upside down to demonstrate that pulp will not slide off.

Step 9
A traditional mould has ribs across the back so that pressure spreads evenly across its entire surface.
For the same effect with a simple mould, push on the screen area with fingers or. . .

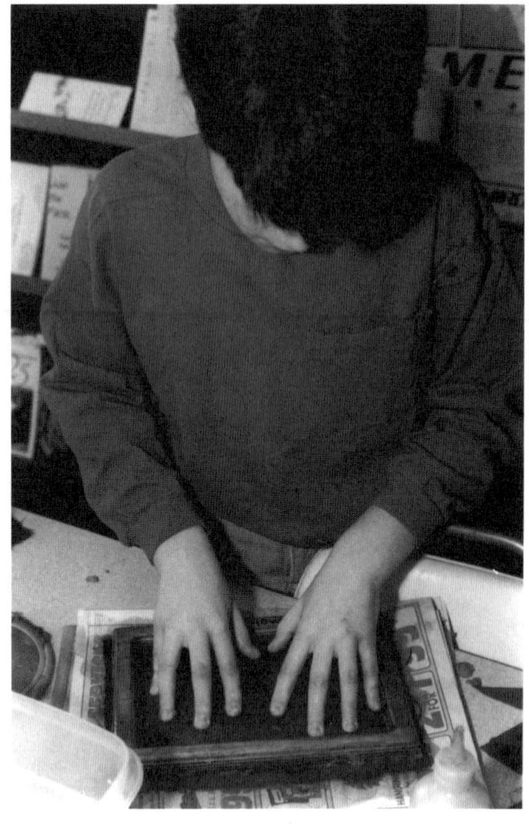

. . . use a sponge, both of which help attach the pulp to the felt and release it from the mould.
Using sponges is great in classrooms, for especially excited children who are in much too much of a hurry to "bother" letting the mould drain.

Next, pick up the mould, starting at an edge or a corner, and slowly "roll" it up and away from the paper. (See photo on opposite page.) If the mould does not release, lay it down and press on the screen again. Sometimes, if the felt is dry and the student sponges enthusiastically, the sheet may be too dry and won't release. Gently pour water on the back of the mould to correct the situation.

Once again, we are dealing with the scientific principle of surface tension. Couching is successful when the surface tension on the felt side is higher than on the mould side. To reduce surface tension on the mould side, the back of the mould can either be wet or dry. Neal Bonham explains this concept very well: "Think of your hair when dry or when under water. There is no surface tension to make the fibers cling."

A felt that is too wet may create other problems, including bubbles, wrinkles and tears. (You may need to start over, but if you do, wring out the felt first, because it is probably soaking wet.) Mostly, I tell students not to worry because the press removes bubbles. With practice, couching technique improves, so fewer and fewer bubbles are created.

If a sheet on the felt cannot be salvaged, remove it by folding the felt over and pressing the pulp together. The pulp acts like a magnet, sticking together upon each folding, until the glob of pulp can be picked up in your hand and tossed back into the vat or recycled in the blender. Obviously, if you toss the

Step 9
Pick up mould by starting at an edge or corner, rather than lifting the entire mould at once. "Roll" the mould up and away from the paper to help avoid bubbles, wrinkles and tears.

lump in the vat, it may not be stirred in as completely as if the pulp went into a blender, so your chances of forming smooth sheets is lessened. However, in order to preserve teacher sanity in the classroom, you may need to give up the goal of having each student form a perfect sheet.

After the sheet is formed and couched, it is ready to be tagged (see Chapter Five, "Special Tips for Teachers") and stacked, one on top of another, before putting it into the press.

If students are going to put more imagery on their paper, using some of the techniques described in Chapter Four, be sure to emphasize that they must carry their felt on top of a newspaper at all times. I allow students to move about the classroom, so they have an opportunity to use a variety of colors. However, they must have their felt next to the vat they are working from, and they can only move their felt from vat to vat if they carry it on top of a stack of newspapers. Not only does such a precaution help keep the floor dry, but sheets are less likely to wrinkle and tear.

If movement in the classroom is too much to tolerate, assign students to a table and provide whatever colors you can. Don't worry, your young papermakers will still enjoy the process!

A NON-STEP *(I hope!)*

Occasionally, this step may need to be part of the papermaking process. When a very poor sheet is formed and needs to be removed from the mould, show the students the technique called "kissing off." (The minute you say "kissing off," you will have the complete attention of every child in the classroom!)

Step 10
When sheets are finished, students place name tags on them and carry them to the press. INSIST that papers–on–felts are carried on top of newspapers to avoid dripping.

After pressing, a sheet is strong enough to be gently picked up.

Simply turn over the mould and lay it on the surface of the water. ***Don't submerge it.*** When water covers the screen, lift the mould and the screen will be pulp–free. Then, be sure to stir the pulp well before forming another sheet.

STEP 10 • *Pressing the paper*

When using a press, stack the felts one on top of the other. This stack of felts is called a "post." Place a dry felt on the top of the post and center it in the press. After applying pressure, leave the stack in the press, if possible, for about 10 minutes. Releasing the pressure causes the moisture to wick back from the felts into the paper; for this reason, sheets pressed for a shorter period of time won't be as dry. "Good" felts wick water from the paper, leaving it fairly dry. See Chapter One, "Tools," for more information about presses and pressing.

STEP 11 • *Drying the paper*

See Chapter One, "Tools," for information on various ways to dry the paper.

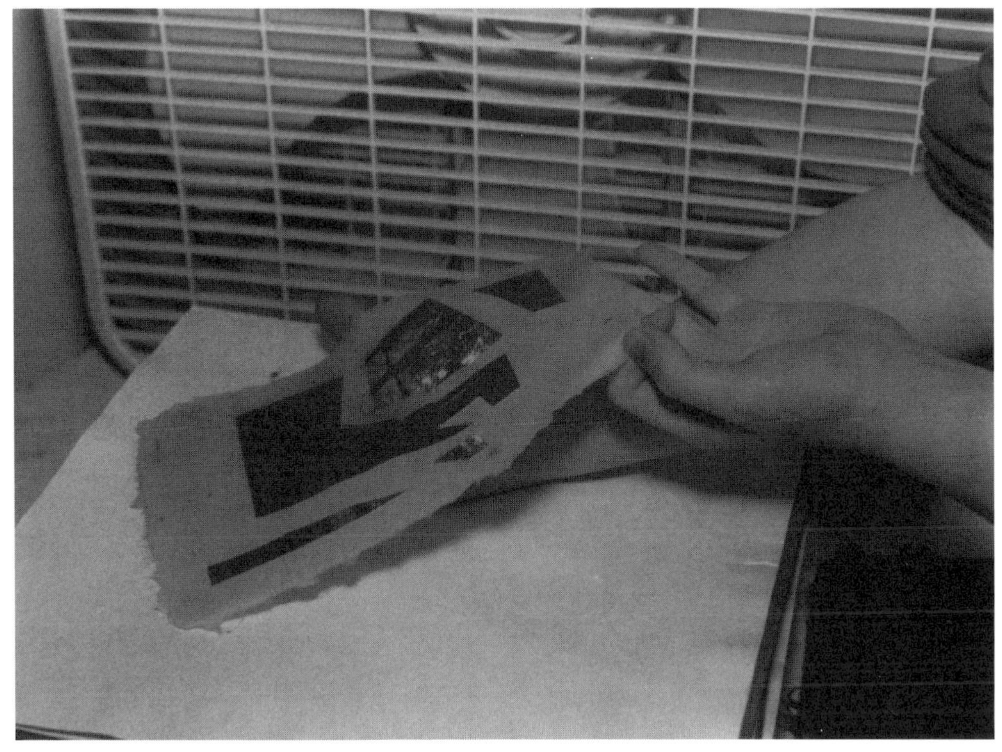

Placing damp, pressed paper in stack dryer

Placing layer of blotter paper on wet sheet of handmade paper. When damp paper is completely loaded into stack dryer, put weight on top and turn on fans.

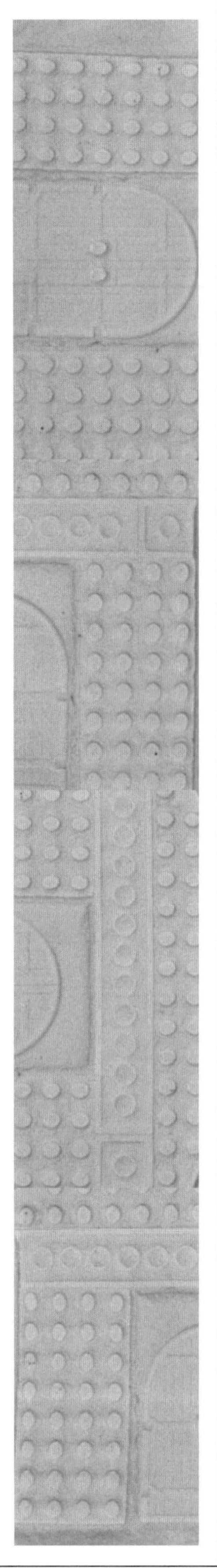

Chapter Four

Pulp as an Art Medium

The art of papermaking is very ancient. What's new about hand papermaking is not only is pulp used to make sheets of paper, but pulp is being manipulated in a wonderful variety of ways as a medium with which to create art. Examples include pressing pulp into a mold to make paper sculpture or using finely beaten pulp in squeeze bottles to draw or paint images. Papermakers are discovering more and more ways that pulp can be manipulated. Several techniques are presented in this chapter. Perhaps you and your students will develop some techniques of your own!

FOUND AND MADE STENCILS

Imagery with pulp can be created by using stencils. A deckle is, in a sense, a stencil. You can purchase different shaped deckles from suppliers to make various shaped papers, such as circles and ovals. You can also easily make your own deckles or stencils in several ways using inexpensive materials.

Lay stencil on top of mould and dip mould into pulp

Paper Stencils • To make a stencil, simply cut a piece of paper the size of the mould and cut your stencil out of that paper. Paper stencils are useful for limited applications.

Advantages of paper stencils are the low cost, the quickness with which they can be made, and the opportunity to encourage each student's creativity by making an original stencil.

The disadvantage, of course, is that paper stencils eventually fall apart. Some kinds of paper are more durable and more water resistant than others, and eventually, you will find the kinds of paper which work best for you.

Encourage simplicity for beginners, since complex stencils, especially ones with small details, are more difficult to work with.

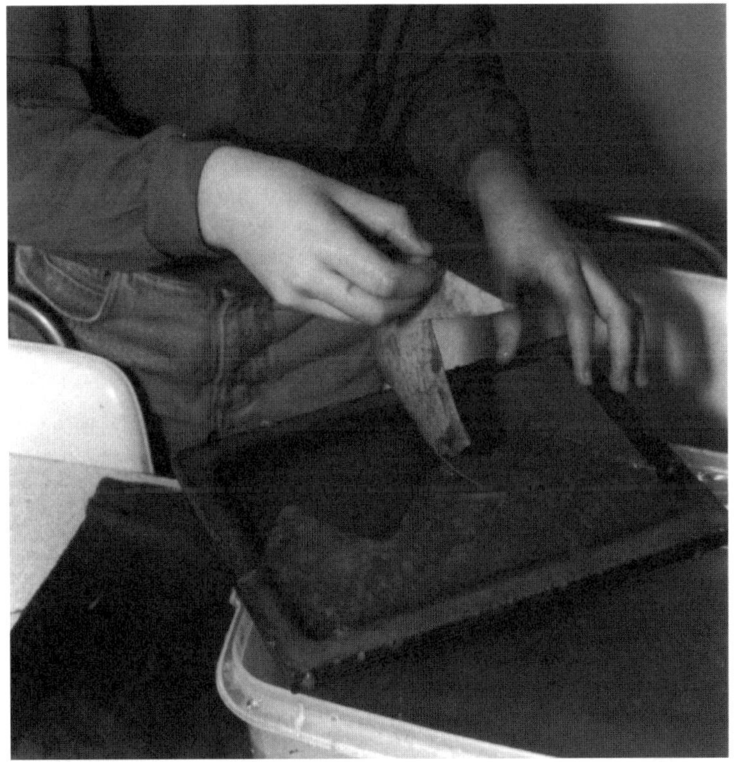

Remove stencil

When using the stencil to create imagery, start by forming a base sheet of paper and couching it on a felt. Next, put the paper stencil on top of the mould. Dampen the paper stencil on both sides to help it adhere to the mould. Dip the mould in the pulp (a deckle is optional — it may help, but sometimes, it just gets in the way), remove the stencil and couch the paper on your base sheet, which laminates the two pieces together.

Pulps with shorter fibers work better with stencils because the fibers don't overlap onto the stencil, making its removal from the screen difficult. Recycled pulp is great for stencils!

Laminating stenciled pulp image onto previously formed sheet

Pulp laminates to base sheet when mould is removed

Found Stencils • Plenty of existing objects can be used for stencils. Encourage observation and creativity in using objects for multiple purposes by asking students to find their own items that may work as stencils.

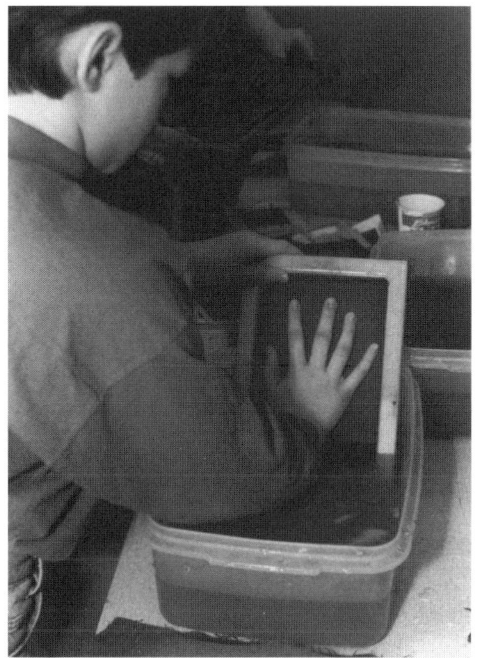

Encourage creativity and observation to find existing objects for stencils

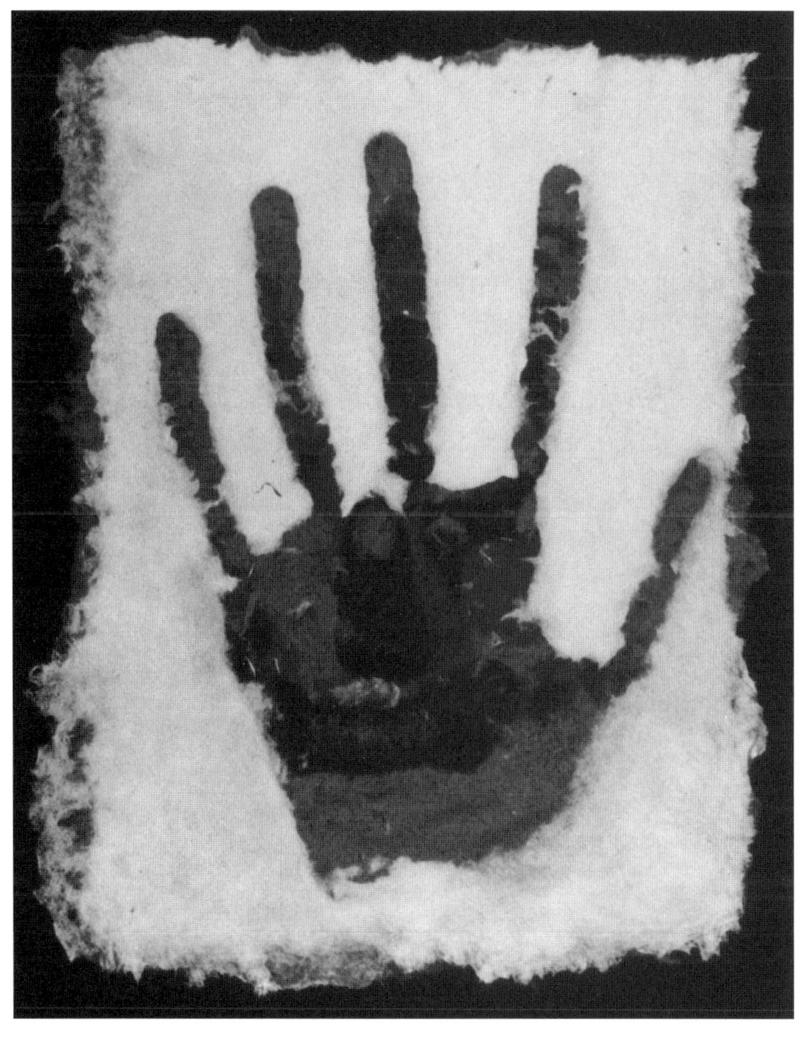

Paper from cookie cutter stencils

Use a more waterproof material, such as Naugahyde, for much-used stencils.

Create an envelope stencil by unfolding a paper envelope and tracing its outline.

Cookie Cutter Stencils • Cookie cutters which are open on top and bottom make great stencils. Place the cookie cutter on the mould, scoop some pulp into a small container and pour the pulp into the cookie cutter until the screen is covered with pulp. Let the mould drain for a moment before removing the cookie cutter. Turn the mould over and couch the image onto the base sheet. To prevent puddles on the floor when making stencil images, be sure to use sponges when couching the paper.

Stencils for Repeated Use • If stencils are to be used many times, make them from a material more waterproof than paper. When I discovered that the Naugahyde which was to cover the seats of my kitchen chairs worked well, it became stencils before I ever had a chance to cover the chairs! Neal Bonham suggests that stencils made of porous materials (e.g. pellon, screen, or thin foam) allow the water to go through, which sometimes gives better pulp control. Styrofoam meat trays make great stencils and reinforce the value of finding new uses instead of throwing materials into landfills. Students learn best from our example.

SHAPED–SCREEN LAMINATING

Equipment • See Chapter One, "Tools," for information on creating duct–tape/aluminum screen moulds in various shapes. Your choice of screen shapes may be influenced by a particular theme, such as buildings. Use these moulds for the laminating technique in this section.

Creating your own screens may be a challenge best undertaken by a small group working with you after school. Because patience and good craftsmanship are needed to evenly tape the edges of the screen so the moulds will last for any length of time, my success with groups making their own screens during classes has been limited. Most students (both adults and children!) try to rush the taping process and then the moulds do not hold up well.

Pulp • Pulps with short fibers, such as cotton linter or recycled pulps, work best for shaped–screen printing. Pulps with longer fibers extend over the edges of the tape, making it more difficult to create the image you want.

At least three colors of pulp should be available for this project. Keep the pulp used for the shaped screens fairly thin. Too much pulp on the screen may flow onto the tape and give a less defined image.

Make duct tape/aluminum screen moulds in many shapes to create papers of different shapes or to laminate images of pulp onto paper

Using a duct tape/aluminum screen mould; these moulds are used without a deckle.

Laminating shaped–screen image to base sheet

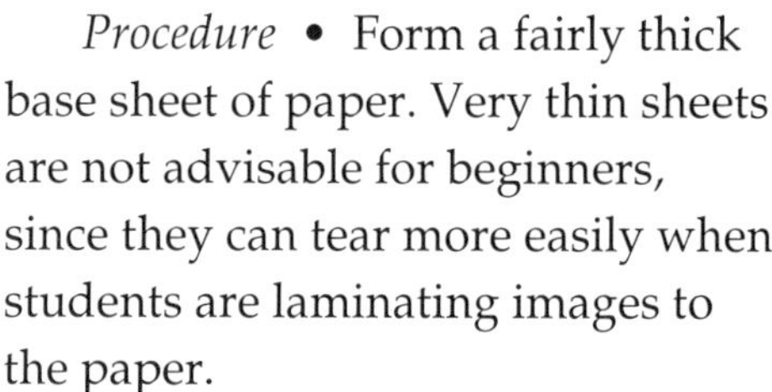

Procedure • Form a fairly thick base sheet of paper. Very thin sheets are not advisable for beginners, since they can tear more easily when students are laminating images to the paper.

Next, dip a small screen into the pulp and bring it out when it is covered. Encourage students to dip the shaped screen rather shallowly. After dipping, using fingers to remove excess pulp from the tape helps keep the image well–defined.

Turn over the screen onto the wet base sheet. Laminate the image onto the base sheet by pushing on the SCREEN part of the mould, not the taped part. Then, gently lift the screen away from the paper. The image remains on the base sheet.

"Incognito Mosquito" by Mandi Ballantyne age 14

Shaped–screen laminating

EMBEDDING

Embedding, a technique for incorporating objects into the paper, can be done in several different ways.

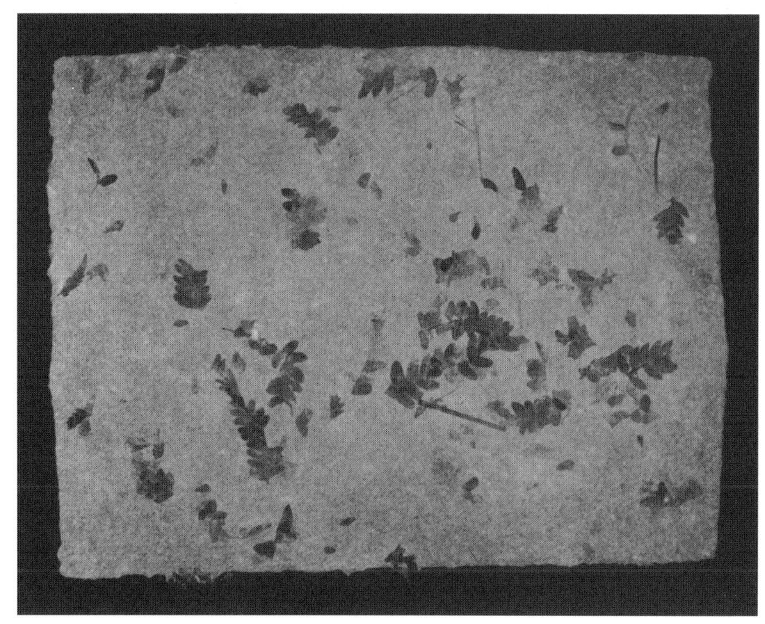

Small object embedding: fern paper

SMALL OBJECT EMBEDDING

Nearly any small item, such as glitter, coffee grounds, tea leaves, spices, flower petals, pieces of thread, or grasses can be added to the pulp in the vat. When you "pull" a sheet, these objects are mixed with the pulp and become embedded in the sheet.

LARGE OBJECT EMBEDDING

Large objects can be embedded in one of two ways.

Partial Embedding • A large object, such as a feather, can be embedded by first laying it on a newly formed sheet. Next, scoop some pulp with a small screen. Laminate the pulp to the sheet by covering only part of the object.

Partial embedding: two fabric triangles can be incorporated into the piece of paper by covering one edge of the triangles with pulp

"Thin veil" embedding: placing cut-up photograph on base sheet of paper

Covering base sheet and cut-up photograph with thin sheet of abaca

Image shows through pulp after removing mould

As the paper dries, it becomes less transparent, but the embedded image will still be fairly clear if a thin enough layer of pulp was used for the cover sheet.

"Thin Veil" Embedding • To completely embed large objects, such as photographs or flowers, under a layer of pulp, a very small amount of pulp relative to the amount of water is needed in the vat. With its long fibers and its ability to make extremely thin sheets, abaca works particularly well for embedding.

If it is important that your felts do not become stained, test the objects being embedded for color-fastness before you embed them, or develop an alternative felt, such as a folded towel.

First, form a base sheet of paper. Next, place the chosen object on it. Now, form another sheet, using as little pulp as possible. Remember, pulp is very transparent when wet, so it may seem that very little or no

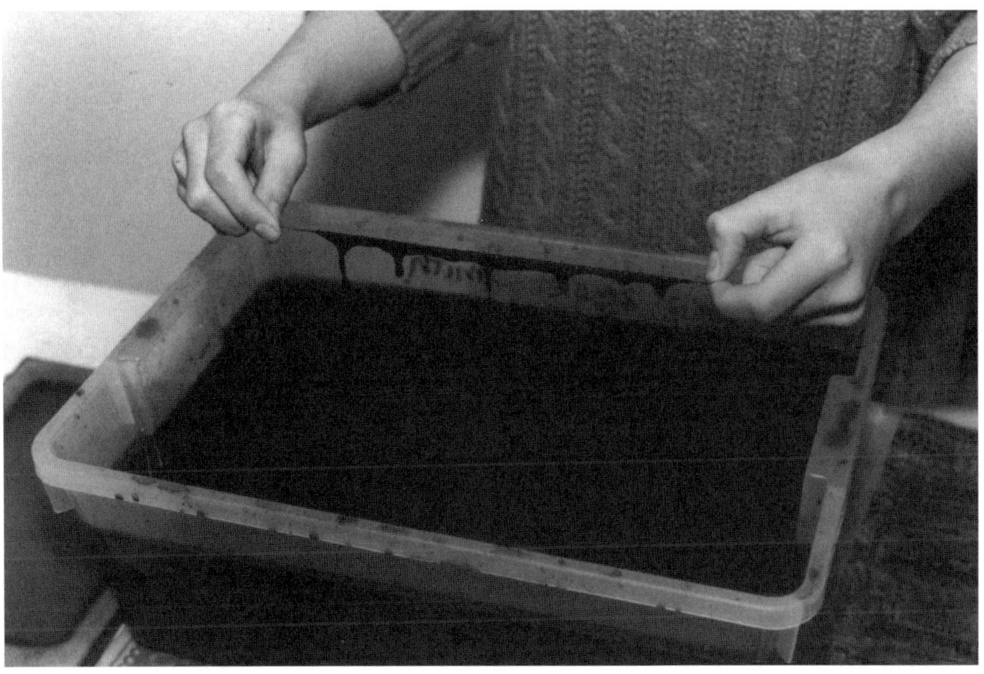

To incorporate threads into a piece of paper, hold threads tautly, dip them into pulp vat . . .

pulp is on the mould, but fibers DO remain. Couch this very thin sheet onto the base sheet and object. Remember that when the paper dries, the sheet will be much less transparent, and the embedded object will not be nearly as visible as when the paper is wet.

After the sheet is pressed and dried, the sheet can be made even more transparent by coating it with a diluted acrylic medium, thinned with water, using the ratio of one part acrylic medium to four parts water. Apply this solution to the paper with a brush and allow it to dry.

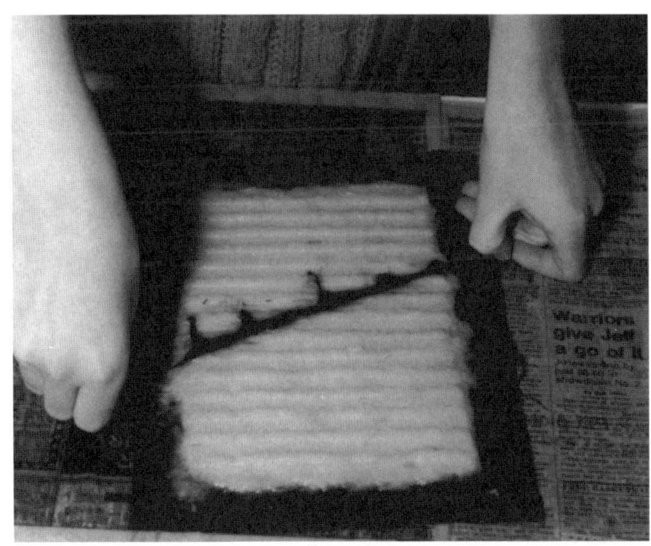

. . . and embed them into the paper by laying them on base sheet

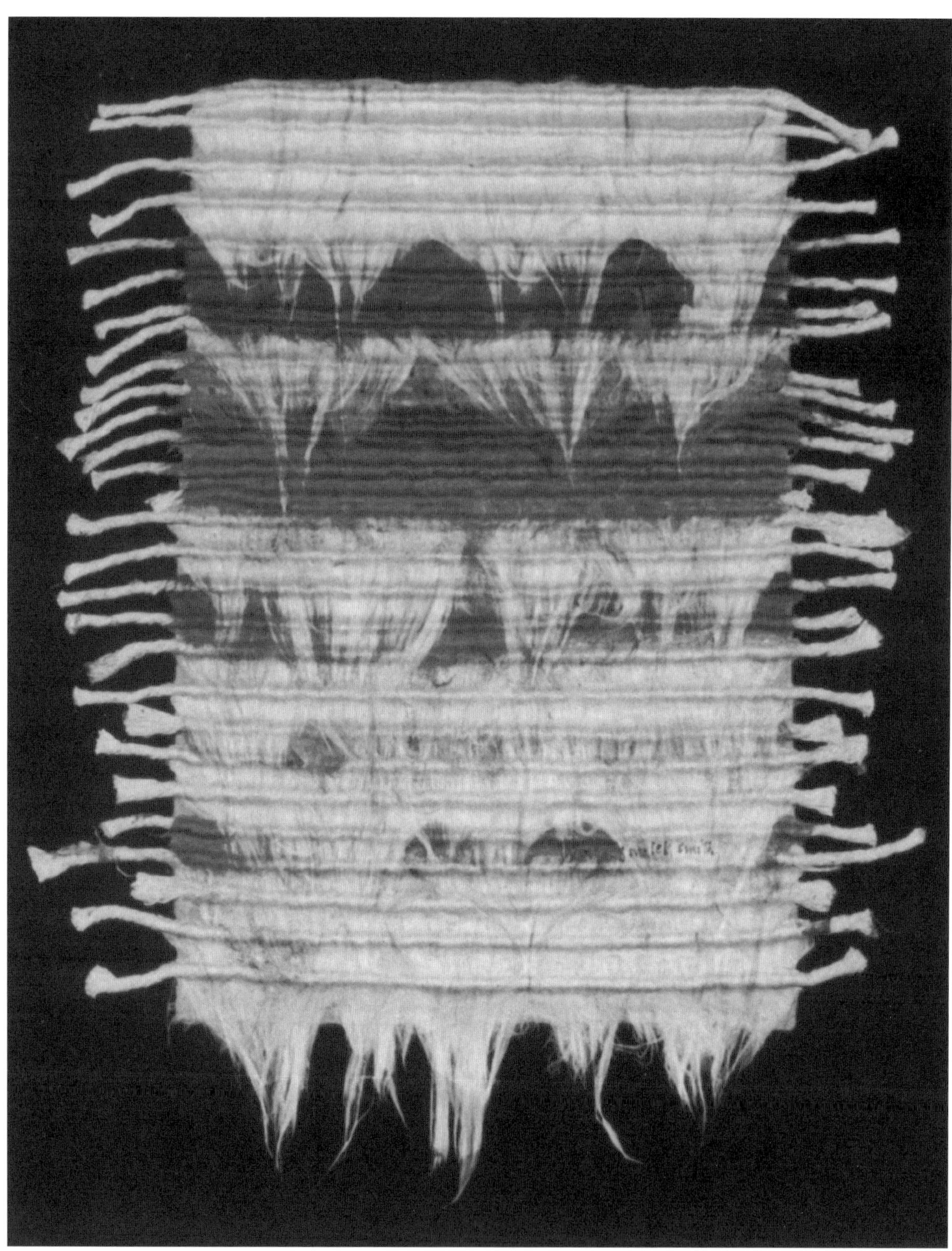

Embedding: kozo weaving by the author

EMBOSSING

Embossing makes indentations in wet paper. Because the paper is wet when embossing is done, all the details of the embosser are picked up on the paper surface.

Choice of Pulp • Any type of pulp may be used for embossing. However, pulps with short fibers, such as cotton linter or recycled paper, tend to give finer detail. The paper's thickness is also important. Generally, thicker paper gives a better embossed impression. To make thicker paper, put more pulp in the vat when forming sheets or laminate several thin sheets together. Laminate by laying one wet sheet on top of another wet sheet. When pressed together and dried, the thin sheets bond and form one single sheet.

Embossers • An embosser may be almost anything. However, objects that are relatively flat work best, because they can remain on the paper while the sheet is in the press and the stack dryer, creating a sharper image. Examples of good embossers are coins, needlepoint plastic canvas, string, rick–rack, LEGOS™, and lace. Show students a few examples and they should be able to find usable objects from home.

Procedure • The procedure for embossing is quite straightforward. First, form a sheet of paper. Next, lay the embosser(s) on top, and leave them on while placing the paper in the press. Extra felts may be added between papers in the press to

Embossing: pressing textured surface into pulp

House image created by embossing LEGOS™ on a sheet of newly formed paper before pressing

prevent transferring the embossed image from one student's paper to another. Keeping the embosser in place while the paper dries is not mandatory, but leaving it on the paper through the drying process usually results in a more distinct image. Remove the embosser when the paper is dry.

THREE–DIMENSIONAL CASTING

One way that paper can take on a third dimension is by casting it in three–dimensional molds.

Made Molds • Rather than restating information about three–dimensional mold–making, I'll refer you to two good sources. Bernard Toale's book, *The Art of Papermaking*, contains a fine chapter about plaster–casting. More detailed information about mold–making can be found in Arthur Williams' *Sculpture: Technique-Form-Content*.

Found Molds • For beginning papermakers and younger students, found molds are the easiest to use. For large classes where many molds are needed, you can save time, money and storage space, by showing students examples of found molds and asking them to bring their own.

It's helpful for the molds to be impervious to water, so kitchen items are most useful. (The mold shown in the photograph is a pan for baking cornbread which I picked

Casting: Form and press a thick sheet of paper to place in mold. . .

This "found" mould was purchased for 25–cents at a garage sale. After showing students some examples, you can assign them to bring their own molds for three–dimensional casting projects.

. . . then, place fiberglass screen over pulp and apply pressure with sponge or brush to push pulp completely into mold and remove moisture.

up for twenty–five cents at a garage sale.) Encourage the use of metal and plastic so you don't have to worry about breakage.

Bowls work well and are readily available. Casting on the inside of the bowl makes the paper easier to remove, but casting can also be done on the outside surface.

Candy molds are fun, and cookie cutters with backs can be used. Objects cast with small molds, such as cookie cutters, dry quicker, require much less pulp and less storage space while drying. Clay cookie molds are great, but they are expensive, breakable and not all parents are willing to let children bring them to school.

New masks can be made by casting on positive molds. Use existing Halloween masks as molds or make a mask without an existing mask for a mold by first creating a base mask with clay. The clay

When completely dry, remove pulp from mold

should be wet enough to be easily manipulated and yet dry enough to push against without quickly losing its shape. Cover the clay with plastic wrap and cast the paper onto the plastic–covered clay. Remove the paper when dry and the clay can be reused.

As you encourage students to look for anything that might serve as a mold, you can help them understand three necessary concepts in order to select appropriate items. The first concept is that of an *undercut* and why it must be avoided. Second, students need to realize that dry paper is much more difficult (if not impossible) to remove from an object with 90–degree angles, like those found on bottles, than from objects with tapered forms, like those found on bowls. Third, an understanding of positive and negative space is essential to three–dimensional casting. For additional information for yourself or for students, refer to the books by Bernard Toale, Arthur Williams or any book on cast sculpture.

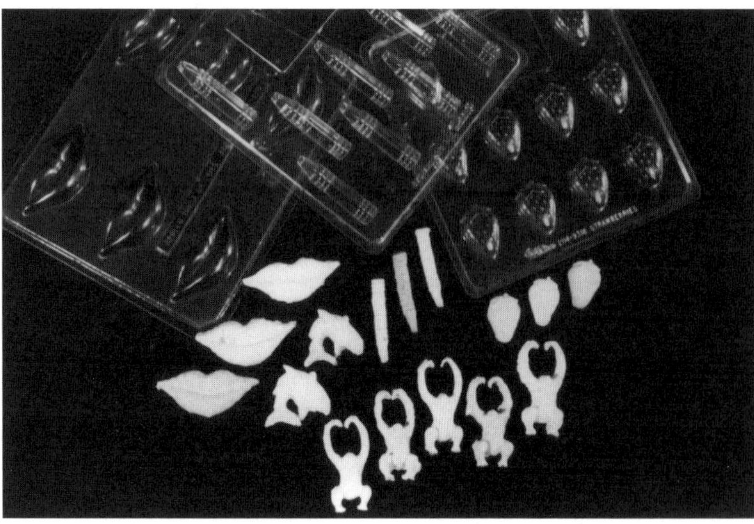

Candy molds used for three–dimensional casting

The paper cast in these molds could be used to make pins, necklaces or earrings, or to become part of an additive sculptural piece.

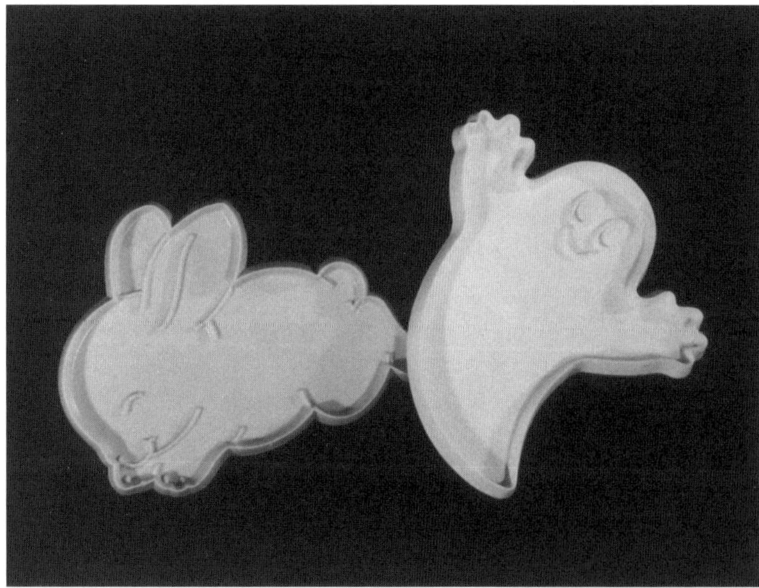

Cookie cutters: "found" molds for three–dimensional casting

Choosing Pulp • Cotton linter is often chosen as a pulp for casting because of its short fibers and its ability to pick up detail. Abaca or flax might be chosen for strength. A mixture of these pulps could create the desired result. Pulp used for casting is usually beaten for a short time, creating a pulp with little shrinkage, so it won't pull away and lose the shape of the mold.

When ordering beaten pulp, be sure to specify that you intend to use the pulp for three–dimensional casting. A small amount of methyl cellulose (an adhesive which can be ordered from papermaking suppliers) may be added to the pulp for strength. Adding too much methyl cellulose makes the pulp stick to the mold. Since most of my projects with children have been small, I have not found it necessary to add methyl cellulose to the pulp.

Kaolin clay may also be added to reduce the shrinkage of paper pulp during drying. As a starting point, try mixing 3 ounces of dry Kaolin clay per pound of dry pulp. Add more clay if necessary.

Preparing Molds • Many books suggest the use of a release agent to keep the paper from sticking to the mold. I rarely use a release agent, but if you have problems with paper sticking to the mold, try using a substance such as vegetable oil spray, liquid dish soap, or green soap. You can also cover your object with plastic food wrap (such as Saran Wrap™).

Plaster molds can be coated with paste wax, polyurethane or varnish to make them more impervious to water, which may also eliminate problems with sticking. However, I have not had any problems with working directly on the uncoated plaster surface. Be aware that paper will not come off the mold easily until it is completely dry. Experience will guide you in knowing when the paper is dry.

Casting Process • Casting may be done in two ways. One is to drain the pulp and apply the pulp directly to the mold. Another way to cast is to form sheets first and then pick up the sheets and apply them to the mold. I prefer the second method for two reasons. One, fiber–to–fiber bonding is improved by forming sheets, and two, it's easier to create more uniform and thinner layers, which reduces drying time.

For the first method, drain the pulp and apply it to the mold, pushing the pulp into the mold, squeezing out water as you press. Imagery can be created by using different colored pulps. When the mold is covered with pulp, sponge out as much moisture as possible. Use fiberglass screening placed over the pulp to protect the piece while sponging.

Many students stop sponging after too short a time and leave excessive moisture in their work. Be sure to check their pieces once they think they are finished, as they often need to be encouraged to sponge out more of the moisture. In small areas, use a stencil brush or some other kind of tool to push the pulp into the mold. Pieces which are very wet when set out to dry require extended drying time and may not be as strong because the fibers will not be pushed together well. Very wet pieces also shrink more and may pull away from the mold, losing the intended shape. Other techniques, such as embossing and embedding may be used in conjunction with casting.

The procedure for the second method is similar, except that sheets of pulp, rather than handfuls, are used. Students should form several thick sheets of paper. Because classroom time is often limited, sheets should be pressed manually by covering the sheets with a fiberglass screen and sponging out the water. (If there is time, the press can be used, but be careful not to get the sheets too dry.)

When sheets are dry enough, pick them up and place them on the mold. Single sheets do not need to cover the entire mold. Small pieces of paper can be overlapped and laminated together. If sheets are thin, several layers may be necessary. Methyl cellulose may be brushed between layers for added strength. Experience will teach you how thick to make layers for various projects.

Wait until the paper is COMPLETELY dry before gently removing it from the casting mold.

PULP PAINTING

Painting with pulp is a process which enables you to use the finely beaten pulp in squeeze to make detailed imagery on your paper.

Materials needed:
Pulp, preferably highly beaten (approximately 4 to 12 hours)
Coloring (pigment or dye)
Formation aid
Plastic squeeze bottles (8–ounce clear, preferred)
Funnel

Pulp • You can try using any kind of pulp, including recycled pulp, but I prefer to use pulp that has been beaten for about four hours. I use both abaca and flax. Other papermakers I know use linen and some use cotton. If you do not have access to a Hollander beater, you might splurge a bit and buy some highly beaten pulp from a supplier. It keeps quite well, especially if you can refrigerate it. Don't freeze it because it gets too lumpy. Order the smallest amount possible — a little goes a long way. Blender pulps offer varying degrees of success.

Coloring • You will be able to make strong bright colors when pigmenting highly beaten pulp. To color pulp, fill one–gallon plastic milk cartons about three–quarters full, add pigment and retention aid, and shake. Refer to pages 24 – 26 for more detailed instructions on how to pigment pulp. (The milk cartons also make a handy way to store this pulp.) When you are ready to use the pulp, put each color of pulp in its own squeeze bottle.

Formation Aid • To help the pulp flow out of the bottle more smoothly, add about a teaspoon of prepared formation aid per bottle. Proportions of pulp and formation aid vary with the concentration of pulp, the concentration of formation aid, and the consistency of pulp with which you like to work. Thin the pulp with lots of water for a wash effect. Very thick pulp makes for more defined images.

Formation aid, available from any papermaking supplier, is commonly used in the vat in Japanese papermaking to keep the long fibers from tangling. Three types are available: PNS, PMP, and PEO. I use both PMP and PEO. They come in powder form and are mixed with water. PEO, which is mixed in the blender, is easier to prepare without lumps, but loses sliminess after time. Because of this, PEO needs to be used fairly soon after mixing, but I have found that refrigeration extends its life.

I often have difficulty mixing PMP without lumps. Marilyn Sward suggests that the powder be dispersed in alcohol before adding water. The PMP needs to be prepared in advance, so it has time to smooth out. If you have remaining lumps, strain the mixture through a colander lined with synthetic organdy. PMP keeps its slimy consistency indefinitely. Since PNS Formation Aid is used only when no other additives (such as color) are used with the pulp, it is not appropriate for this application. However, when PNS is used with colored pulps, it causes the fibers to coagulate or clump, so that colors combined in the vat remain distinct. Decorative papers may be created in this way.

Painting with Pulp • First, form a piece of paper on a felt. Then, "paint" with the different colored pulps on that piece of paper. Be sure students work with a stack of dry newspapers under the felt. Adding more pulp adds more water.

Squeezing pulp out of a bottle is great fun and some students can get carried away, so you may want to offer a few of the guidelines I find useful. I encourage students to make imagery without words or initials. I encourage them to express personalities with color, line, and shape, rather than writing their names or just randomly squirting pulp. I ask students to think about their image before they create it, and remind them that drawing with pulp works best for details and small images they are unable to create in other ways.

Pulp painting

Drying the Sheets • Because the painting pulp has been beaten much longer than the pulp used for base sheets, painting pulp has many more "pieces" of fiber. Because each piece of fiber holds water, the highly beaten pulp is going to hold much more water. When first applied, the painting pulp looks like "puff paint," but as the water drains out, the pulp flattens. When drying, the highly beaten pulp (with more water) shrinks far more than the less–beaten pulp. Therefore, when these two pulps are combined, as in pulp painting, pieces should be dried under restraint (such as a stack dryer) to reduce the amount of warpage. See Chapter One, "Tools," for information on stack dryers.

Alternate pulp painting technique II: removing pulp from screen to form image

ALTERNATE PULP PAINTING TECHNIQUE I

Mina Takahashi and Helen Hiebert of Dieu Donné Papermill use a different technique for pulp painting in their childrens' classes. They add formation aid and methyl cellulose to their pulp to create a pulp mixture that can be actually manipulated with paint brushes instead of squeeze bottles. Gertrude Simon suggests that the pulp can also be applied using a spoon.

Beginning to laminate image onto previously formed base sheet

ALTERNATE PULP PAINTING TECHNIQUE II

Images can be drawn with the pulp in another way. First, form a base sheet of paper and couch on a felt. Next, using a different color of pulp from a vat, "pull" a second sheet. Remove the deckle and use fingers to remove the negative spaces of the image by pushing around and removing pulp from the mould. When the image is ready, turn the mould over and laminate the image onto the base sheet.

Laying down small piece of pulp to form eye

Final image: "Ruff"

Traditional watermark made with embroidery floss on a picture frame/windowscreen mould

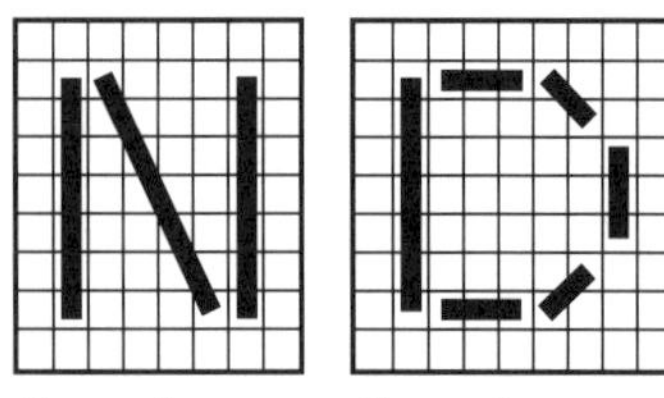

Figure A Figure B

Embroidery watermark patterns

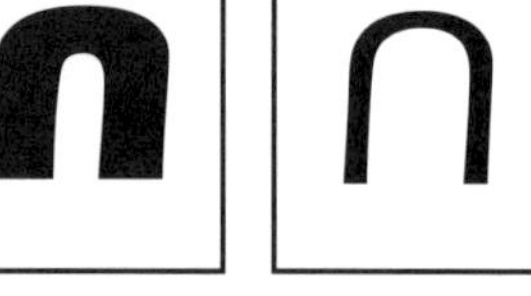

Figure C Figure D

For foam shadowmarks, broader shapes (C) do not work as well as narrower shapes (D)

WATERMARKS

Watermarks are traditionally made by attaching a wire, either by sewing or soldering, to the screen surface of the mould. During sheetforming, the pulp settles in a thinner layer over the slightly raised area of the wire. When the sheet of paper is held to the light, the image formed by the wire can be seen. A more elaborate type of watermark, often called a shadowmark, is made by embossing the screen of the mould.

A simplified method for the classroom, suggested by Marna Elyea Kern in her book *The Complete Book of Handcrafted Paper*, uses embroidery floss in place of wire.

Embroidery Floss Watermark • To make an embroidery floss watermark, begin by threading a needle with unseparated floss. Tie a knot at one end of the floss which is big enough so the floss does not pass through the opening in the screen. Bring the needle up through the bottom of the screen to start your watermark. To make straight lines, use one long stitch (Figure A). For curved lines, use a series of small straight stitches (Figure B). See the diagram for a better understanding of the stitching technique.

When you have completed the stitching for your watermark, tie another knot on the underside of the screen and cut off the end of the floss.

To make embroidery floss watermarks in a classroom without needing separate moulds for each student, individual watermarks can be made by students on separate pieces of fiberglass window screen, which can then be stretched across an embroidery hoop mould.

Shadowmarking • A new technique for shadowmarking, using non–traditional and inexpensive materials, has been developed by Neal Bonham of Sea Pen Press and Papermill in Seattle. For more detailed information about this technique, please refer to the article "An Interview with Neal Bonham," in *Hand Papermaking*, Volume 9, Number 1, Summer 1994.

Following is a simplified adaptation of Bonham's shadowmarking technique for the classroom. This technique takes a certain amount of patience, and for that reason, it is best suited to high school students. However, if you are able to work with students in small groups, it can also be done with elementary and middle school children.

Beyond standard papermaking equipment, you need 1/16–inch to 1/4–inch thick polyurethane foam, which probably can be found in your local fabric or craft store. Before using the foam, you may find it helpful to wash it in water and detergent and soak it for at least 24 hours.

Cut a sheet of foam the size of the surface of your mould. With another piece of foam, cut out the watermark shape you wish to use, taking care to taper the edge outward to avoid vertical or undercut edges, which tend to trap air bubbles. By avoiding broad spaces on your shape (Figures C and D),

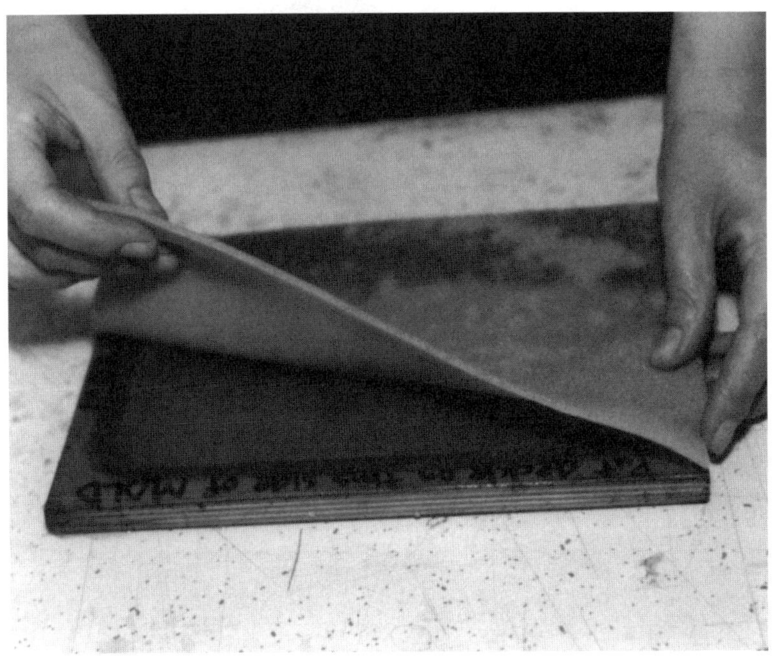

***Shadowmarking:* cut thin foam same size as mould and place it, soaking wet, on mould**

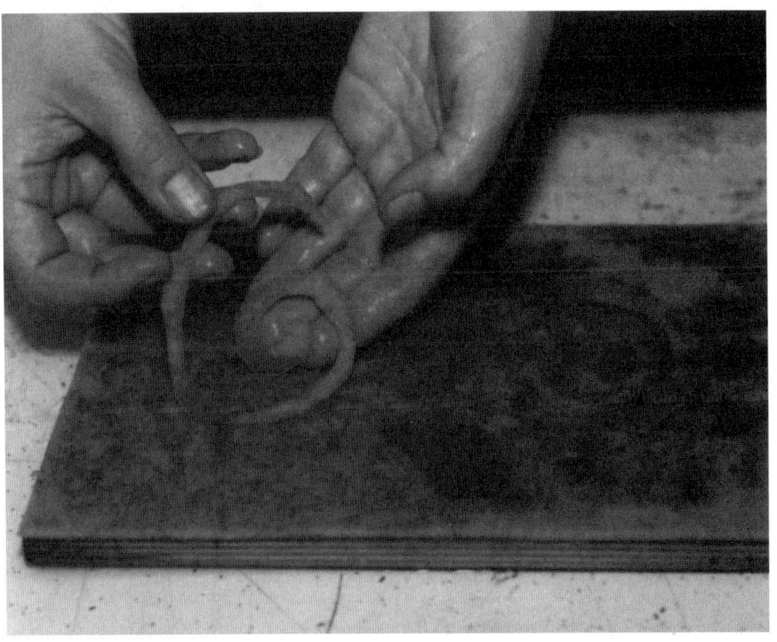

Place soaking wet watermark foam shapes on foam sheet

Dip mould into highly beaten pulp and allow to drain

Dip mould again, this time into moderately beaten pulp, and allow to drain

Roll foam sheet onto wet felt

you can help the mould drain more easily, creating clearer images.

You should prepare two colors of pulp. Neal Bonham uses cotton rag pulp. I have successfully used abaca and flax pulp. One color should be of pulp that is highly beaten (approximately 4–5 hours). The other color can be from pulp that is more moderately beaten (approximately 1–2 hours).

The highly beaten pulp should be a very dilute solution, since you will use it to make a very thin layer of pulp. The other pulp should be the consistency you would use for standard sheetforming.

You also need a vat of water for soaking the foam.

First, soak the large foam sheet and place this WET sheet of foam on your mould.

Next, place the WET foam watermark shapes on the foam sheet. Then, very gently, dip the mould into the vat of highly beaten pulp, taking care to avoid moving the unsecured watermark. Be patient — keeping everything in its proper place takes some practice! Let the mould drain.

Next, dip your mould in the vat of moderately beaten pulp and let it drain very thoroughly, tilting the mould at an angle, if needed. Remove the deckle.

Carefully lift the foam sheet off the mould and roll it onto a wet felt.

(You could also try couching the sheet while the foam is still on the mold. Experiment and use whatever method works best for you.)

Next, peel the foam away from the paper. If you are having problems releasing the foam from the paper, try pouring some water on the back of the foam. Again, this technique takes practice.

Finally, using a tweezers, gently remove the foam shapes from the sheet of paper.

Peel foam away from paper

• NOTE •

If keeping the cut–out shapes in place is a continual problem, you might prefer to glue the foam shapes to the large foam sheet. Five–minute epoxy is the easiest adhesive to use, although 2–hour epoxy creates a more waterproof bond. Use a small spatula to apply the glue as you would spread butter on bread.

Using tweezers if necessary, remove foam shapes from sheet of paper

Finished shadowmarked paper

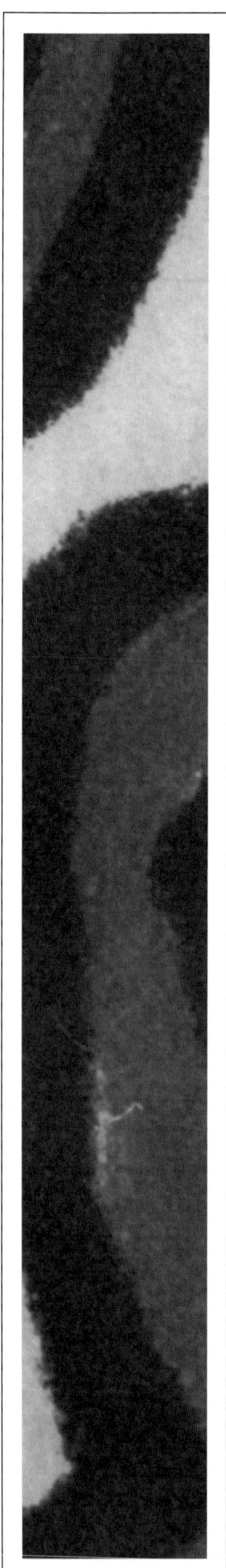

Chapter Five

Special Tips for Teachers

As any teacher certainly knows, it is impossible to teach without learning at the same time. The following chapter contains ideas I have learned about helping papermaking classes to operate smoothly, suggestions for framing handmade paper and, finally, possibilities for field trips.

LESSON PLANNING TIPS

One of the most important things I have had to learn is to introduce the concepts of papermaking slowly. There are many steps in making a piece of paper and students can only grasp so much at a time. So I suggest breaking up the process into as many steps as possible.

Perhaps, the first day is on preparing pulp. The next day might be forming, pressing, and drying the sheets. Ideally, students can practice making several sheets of paper before they advance into using the pulp as a medium.

Of course, few classrooms are ideal, so you must adapt each lesson to suit your particular needs. If you are teaching papermaking without any volunteer help and the class is large, consider creating a papermaking "learning center." The majority of students could work on individual, independent projects at their tables, while each day, a few students go to the learning center and make paper until everyone in the class has a chance at papermaking.

Since students often learn more when put into the role of teacher, those who have already made paper could serve as instructors for students who follow. Many of the ideas throughout this book may be used as individual lessons. In addition, several books cited in the bibliography have useful projects.

Especially for beginning papermakers, I strongly believe that the value of the process is more important than the product, so I caution you against being too project oriented at the outset.

A common question I am asked by parents and teachers is: "After students make their paper, what will they do with it or what will they make with it?" For almost every student, I find that making a piece of paper is very exciting and magical; they feel no need to find a practical use for the sheet. The experience, in and of itself, along with their actual piece of paper, however humble, is totally satisfying to them.

RECRUITING VOLUNTEERS

When teaching papermaking, parent volunteers are a wonderful addition to your classroom. With the many steps involved in the process, an extra pair of hands to help at the press, to help at the stack dryer, and to help individual students who are having problems forming or couching sheets is extremely helpful.

Usually, parents are as much in awe of the papermaking process as the kids are! It's a wonderful chance for them to see a group of enthusiastic children in the art classroom. The best way to show the community that art class is more than "glorified recess" and that serious learning is taking place is to have a few members of the community witness it for themselves.

Although families where both parents work outside the home make it difficult to find volunteers these days, they are out there! Have aprons ready for the wonderful parents who can take an hour or two away from work to volunteer in your classroom. Then, when you need some financial assistance or other help from the PTA, parents know you and are likely to support your projects. Remember, too, that older students make wonderful assistants when working with young children.

KEEPING DRY

Keeping dry is one of the biggest problems when teaching large groups. The method I find works best, even in carpeted rooms, is to have each student work with a felt on a stack of dry newspapers, 3 to 4 sheets thick, at all times. Slick advertising paper should be removed, since it does not absorb water as well and creates a difficult work surface for students.

A typical newspaper section can have as many as 30 layers when folded. If an entire newspaper is used, I like to have the sections opened up, pulled apart and then refolded, so that each one is only two or four layers thick. However, I do this only when I have a group of students to help me with this time–consuming task. The advantage to separating the newspapers is that fewer layers get wet at one time, so not as many newspapers are needed.

Newspapers can be reused if you have a drying rack for prints. By putting wet newspapers in the rack and using a fan to blow air through it, the papers dry quickly. One grocery bag of newspapers is needed for an average classroom (about 25 students) for a 45–minute class.

Put two to four sponges at each table for couching. Use an ice cream bucket (I like to call them "portable sinks") on each table where students can squeeze the excess moisture from their sponges.

Finally, ask parents to donate old towels to have ready if the occasional "big spill" occurs.

To prevent mildew, felts should be dried each day. Felts may be laid out on the tables, across the backs of waterproof chairs, or hung on a clothesline to dry.

If your classroom is like most I find, and is without a clothesline, you may want to add this inexpensive and useful item. Just determine the classroom area with the least amount of traffic and ask the school custodian to install two screw eyes, one each on opposing walls. Attach the clothesline rope, and you're ready to roll. If you don't mind the appearance and it's out of the way, the clothesline can be left hanging or it's easy enough to put up and take down as needed.

WORKING SMALL

. . . or Work Small, Work Sane. . .

To keep your papermaking project more manageable, make paper that is relatively small. Generally, 5-1/2" x 8-1/2" is a good size. To make bigger paper requires bigger moulds. Bigger moulds require bigger vats, bigger felts, and a bigger press and bigger stack dryer This all takes more space. And bigger sheets of wet paper means more drying time. You get the idea.

If you have smaller classes and longer class periods, working with large sheets is great fun, but being able to provide that kind of experience is rare. Be aware and don't set yourself up for something you can't or may not want to continue.

IDENTIFYING PAPERS

. . . or how to know who made which paper when you have 500 of them stacked on your desk. . .

When students are finished making their sheets, the paper will still be wet, so they cannot identify sheets by writing names on them. Cut one–inch–square pieces of any available plain paper and have students write their names and classrooms on them in pencil.

By placing each student's name tag directly on the wet paper, it adheres to the sheet. When the dry pieces of paper are returned to the students, they can peel away the name tag and sign their piece or write their name on the back, whichever they prefer.

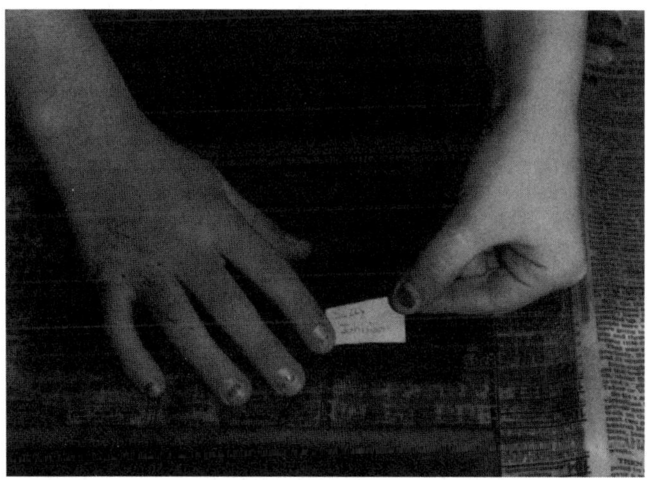

Placing name tag on wet sheet of paper

MOUNTING AND FRAMING

A very simple sheet of paper can be quite elegant when it is either mounted or framed.

Most dedicated art teachers I know and love spend an incredible amount of time mounting and displaying student art work because they know the importance to students of having work displayed. As schools assign more and larger classes to art teachers, finding time to properly display student work becomes more and more difficult.

Here are two suggestions. First, enlist the help of parent volunteers. Hold a training night where a local framer would lend his or her expertise. (Parents could learn some useful skills, the framer could make contacts for future business, and you'll probably create a group of able assistants who could help you both at home and in the classroom.)

Second, teach students to mount and/or frame their own work. Although as a student, I was never taught anything about presenting my art work from elementary grades through graduate school, it certainly would have been helpful.

Again, a community–minded framer may be willing to come to your classroom as a guest speaker.

Matting, mounting, and framing teaches students the value of craftsmanship, an important part of the curriculum, and introduces students to a life skill. Most students will not continue to paint and draw, but many will have several occasions where they need something framed. Following are several suggestions for displaying student work.

Unframed Paperwork • Many paper artists display their work unframed, and it is most appropriate for cast paperwork, thick paper pieces, or paper with strength from particular fibers and their preparation. Because paper is so lightweight, hangers are relatively easy to attach. Even while the paper is being made, a string for hanging could be embedded, or it could be attached after the piece is dry, using glue or tape.

Mounting • The sheet of handmade paper can be mounted on construction paper or matboard. Frame shops throw away tons of small matboard scraps, so acquiring free matboard shouldn't be too difficult. Picking up the matboard scraps might be a task for a parent volunteer who drives by a frame shop every day on the way to work.

While the amount of border for a piece of art work is a matter of personal preference, depending on the size of the piece, my choice for borders range from three to five inches. For example, with a piece of paper 5-1/2" x 8-1/2", use matboard that is 11-1/2" x 14-1/2".

Attach the paper to the mat board by making two hinges out of linen tape. Advantages to attaching handmade paper in this manner are twofold. One is that the paper is not permanently attached to the matboard and if the owner decides to display it in another way, the paper may be removed. The second advantage is in the aesthetic presentation of the paper. Since an interesting and pleasing characteristic of handmade paper is that it is seldom completely as flat as machine–made paper, attaching the paper in just two spots maintains its three-dimensionality.

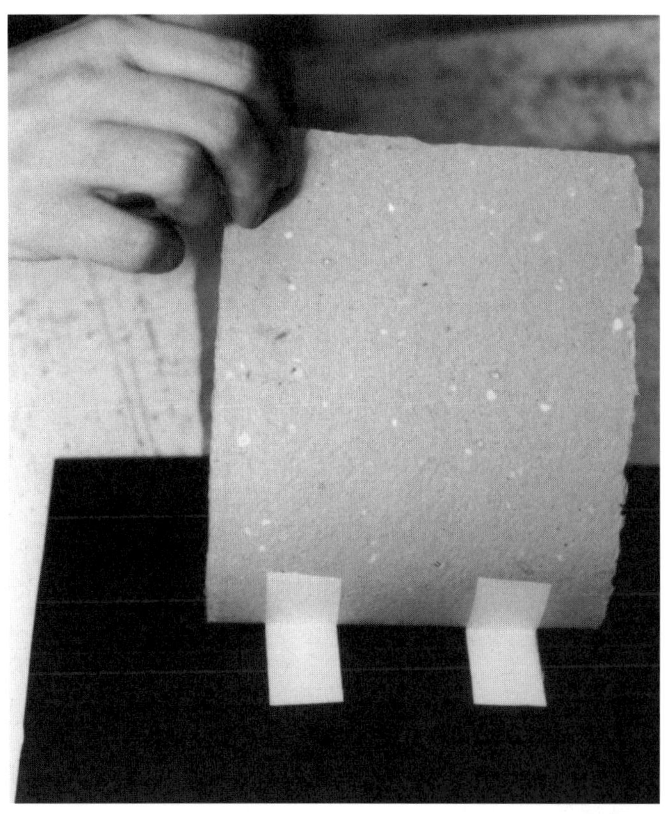

Paper attached to mat board using two hinges of linen tape

Art work mounted on mat board with linen hinges

"Incognito Mosquito" by Mandi Ballantyne age 14

Using foamcore to create depth accommodates the three–dimensionality of handmade paper

Here, the piece of handmade paper is attached to a mat with linen tape. Then a foamcore "frame" is placed on the mat board. Finally, the mat is placed on top of the foamcore.

Mounting and Matting • To present your paper in this manner, follow the directions above for mounting your work, and go one step further by adding a mat. Traditionally, a mat covers the edges of the art work, but when framing handmade paper, the edges of the paper should remain visible because they are unique. Cut the mat so it does not cover the edges of your paper.

Mounting and Matting with Glass and a "frameless" system (Uni–Frame, Braquette or Swiss Clips) • "Frameless" frames are an inexpensive and attractive way to present art work.

When framing art work, the cover glass should not touch the work itself. For most works, a mat provides adequate space between the art work and the glass, but because handmade paper has some dimensionality, more space is often required. Make this space by adding strips of foamcore, or by creating a foamcore "frame" between the mounting board and the mat. Frame shops also throw away foamcore scraps by the ton, so you will do the world a big favor by using some of those scraps in your matting and keeping them out of landfills.

To assemble a "frameless" frame, attach the handmade paper to the mounting board with linen tape.

Next, place the foamcore (which is narrower than the mat, so it remains invisible) on the mounting board, followed by the mat, and finally, the glass. Clips or other brackets hold the assemblage together in what appears to be a "frameless" system.

While few schools have the budget to frame student art work in this manner, if teachers frame a few pieces as examples, parents and students may get ideas for framing their own work with minimal expense.

Mounted art work with mat, ready for "frameless" system or a frame

Frames • Any frame is suitable if it has enough depth for the piece of art work.

Follow the steps above, under Mounting and Matting with Glass and a "frameless" system. When the art work, mounting board, mat and glass are assembled, put them into a frame instead.

Shadowbox frames use deep moulding and are an excellent choice for very thick work. First, the glass is put into the frame. Then, strips of wood are glued on the side of the frame, acting as spacers between the glass and the art work. Next, the art work, mounted on matboard, is placed in the frame. It is not necessary to use a mat when framing work in a shadowbox, but a mat may be used for decorative effect, if desired.

Another option for providing space in frames between art work and glass are purchased spacers, including brand names like Econospace and Framespace. Thin strips of balsa wood can also be used. Finally, metal frames with a built–in spacer can be purchased.

CLASSROOM CLEAN UP

The methods in this book are ones that should help you avoid having lots of clean–up. However, there is always a certain amount of clean–up that must be done.

To facilitate cleaning the equipment, it is helpful to have a large vat of water for students to rinse their screens. Near the rinsing vat, you might have a few towels for patting the screens dry to avoid dripping. When you're finished using the moulds for the day, be sure to clean the screens more thoroughly, by rinsing them off with running water. A garden hose with a nozzle to exert pressure works best.

To avoid plugging the drains with pulp when cleaning screens in the sink, place a square laundry basket (with holes drilled in the bottom and draped with mosquito netting, synthetic organdy, or a similar fabric) in the sink. If your sinks are not large enough to accommodate a laundry basket, try using a large colander.

Keep four or five scrub brushes on hand for students to use when cleaning felts. Because some students are always finished early and need something to do, they can work on this task and have the felts cleaned in no time.

Use a separate container for each type of tool. For example, use one container for cookie cutters, one for shaped screens and so forth, which enables students to help you maintain the organization necessary in a classroom setting.

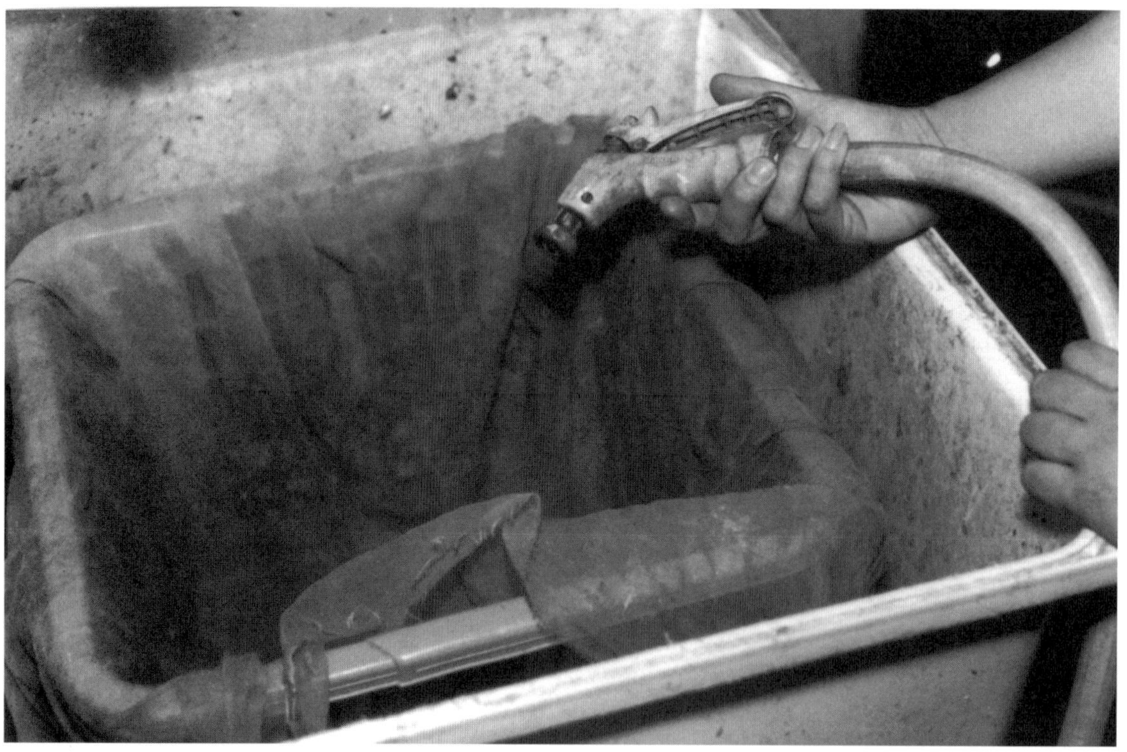

To avoid plugging drains with pulp, use laundry basket "strainer" or colander, lined with synthetic organdy or similar fabric, for clean up

Tour a paper mill

FIELD TRIPS

There are several possibilities for field trips related to the study of hand papermaking. Limitations are created only by the area in which you live.

The ultimate trip would be a visit to the American Museum of Papermaking, located at the Institute of Paper Science and Technology in Atlanta, Georgia. The Museum houses the extensive Dard Hunter Paper Collection. Dard Hunter travelled all over the world, collecting hundreds of papermaking artifacts, including many tools and papers. Exhibitions in the museum show the past, present and future of papermaking.

An exciting field trip would be a visit to Historic Rittenhouse Town, now part of Fairmount Park in Philadelphia, Pennsylvania, and site of the first paper mill in the North American colonies. Rittenhouse Town remained the center of papermaking in America for nearly 100 years after William Rittenhouse began manufacturing paper here in 1690. Special guided tours are available for groups.

Another possibility for a field trip would be touring a local paper mill. Once you have learned how to make paper by hand, it is especially fascinating to see it made by machine.

Related to the paper mill tour is a trip to a cardboard manufacturing factory. Many students are not aware that cardboard is made from paper. Because of safety factors, not all paper factories offer tours to school children, but videotapes of the plant and the papermaking process may be available from them to show to students.

Visits to newspapers, printers, or other places where paper is an essential element of the work would also be appropriate.

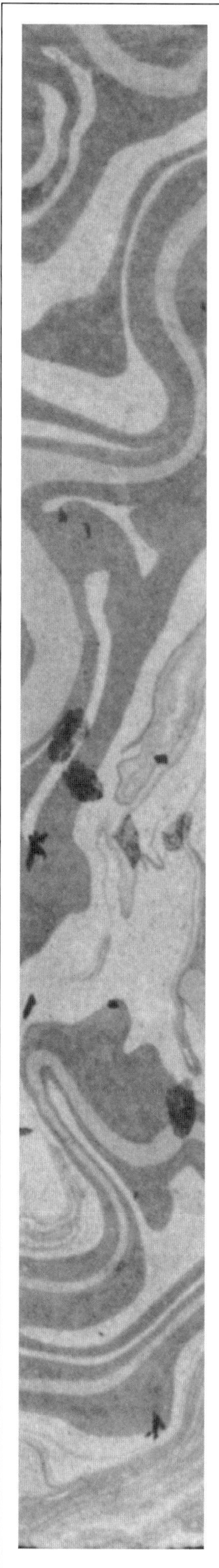

Chapter Six

Integrating Papermaking with the Arts

Papermaking can easily fit into many traditional disciplines taught within the art curricula. More often than not, many artists who are papermakers are using the craft of papermaking in conjunction with other mediums, such as printmaking and photography. One example would be painters using colored pulp instead of paint to make their work.

In the following chapter, I have selected some artistic disciplines and suggested how papermaking might be integrated into the various curricula.

PAINTING: David Hockney Meets Pulp

A good resource for integrating papermaking with art history, reading, photography, and painting is *Paper Pools* by David Hockney.

Hockney's book contains lots and lots of photographs and illustrations. The text is minimal, but offers very good insight on how one artist works. Ideally, you can read the book to the entire class. If that's not possible, try loaning the book to one student at a time, so it can be read in advance of the following assignment.

Once they are familiar with Hockney's book, ask students to concentrate on one idea or topic and then shoot a roll of film with this idea or topic in mind. Students will then translate one or more of their photographs into a pulp painting. If time, cameras or film are not available, students may choose an existing photograph or a part of a photograph and translate it into paper using pulp paint. Encourage them to start with a fairly simple photograph, as it takes time to develop skill with painting pulp. Photographs with lots of detail are more difficult to execute. Refer to David Hockney's example, showing how he starts with a fairly abstract photo, abstracts it further, and then changes it even more to make the final piece pleasing in composition, color, and other artistic values.

Adapt this lesson to a drawing or computer graphics class by starting with drawings or graphic designs students have created themselves and following the process described above.

PRINTMAKING: A Natural Connection

Papermaking and printmaking are connected in a most basic and significant way: the mould is essentially a printing plate whose image is retained by the paper. The screen texture can be seen on the finished pieces of paper. Watermarks, the result of wires attached to the screen, can also be seen. Although there are some subtle differences, relief printing and papermaking are virtually the same reproductive process. Furthermore, paper is necessary for printmaking and the type and quality of the paper plays a major role in the type and quality of the final print.

Handmade paper is suitable for any printmaking project. Printing is possible on both waterleaf (unsized)

Using potato for printing on handmade paper

paper and sized paper. On sized paper, ink sits on top, whereas on waterleaf paper, ink is absorbed into the fibers.

Make some handmade paper to use in your next printmaking project. Students can compare the look of the print on machine–made paper versus handmade paper. Advanced students can create different effects by making the type of paper that is best suited for the finished print they desire.

Many excellent books on printmaking are available, some of which are listed in the Bibliography. In addition, papermaking books often include printmaking projects (see *The Art and Craft of Papermaking* by Sophie Dawson and *Paper Pleasures* by Faith Shannon).

"Land of Blue Hills" by Nathaniel Smith, age 13

Shapes were created by laminating different colored pulps using shaped screens. Detail was added with felt markers.

DRAWING: Another Natural Connection

Drawing is naturally connected with papermaking because the most common surface we use for drawing is paper. The possibilities must be endless, but I'll suggest three ways you can integrate papermaking into a drawing curriculum. Depending on the drawing medium in use, consider adding sizing to the paper. Sizing makes the paper more waterproof and prevents inks and watercolors from bleeding.

Experimental Surfaces • Paper surfaces vary depending upon the type of plant fibers used, by the length of time pulp is beaten, by the quality of the surface the paper is pressed upon, by the method of drying, by adding sizing or not, and so forth. Have students make three different types of paper created using various tools, materials and methods. Then, students can create the same basic drawing on these different surfaces to see how the results vary. Students might use the same medium on each sheet or choose the medium which best suits each paper surface.

Mixed Media: pulp and colored pencil or other suitable media • After making a piece of paper, add imagery with shaped–screen moulds. Once paper has been pressed and dried, use some sort of drawing media to add detail. Drawings can be planned ahead, so that students know what their shapes will become. For example, a cityscape could be created, where buildings are made with rectangular shaped–screen moulds and details like windows are drawn in later.

Combining shaped–screen lamination with drawn–in details could also be approached as a "look at the clouds and see what you see" activity. Initially, students could make the paper, without any preconceived notion or specifications, creating shapes on it. Later, they can be asked to draw in details, using the existing shapes to determine what the final drawing would become.

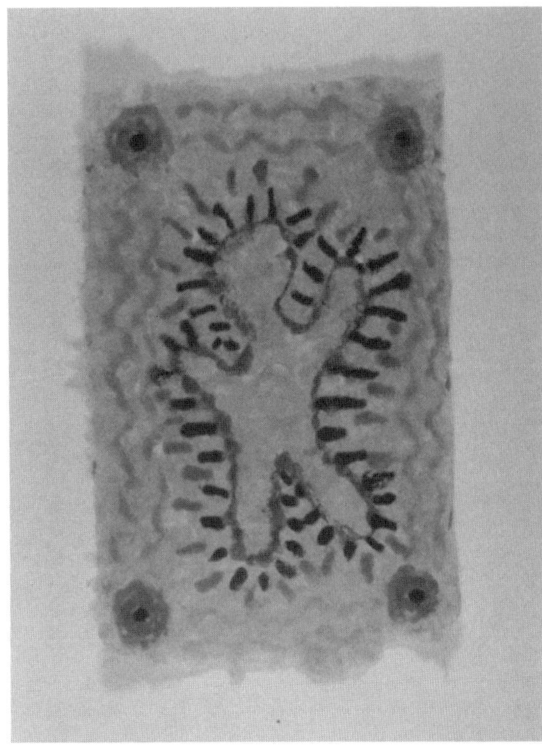

"Cactus Man Jack" by Chandra Jordan grade 12

Image on handmade paper drawn with paint pulp (4–hour beaten abaca) in a squirt bottle

Drawing with Pulp • For drawing, the pulp paint should be reasonably thick. Work from a pencil sketch or make the drawing spontaneously. Start by forming a sheet on the felt. Then, draw on it with the bottled pulp. When the drawing is completed, put it in the press and, finally, dry it under pressure. Remember, because pulp paint is highly beaten, it shrinks a great deal and buckles the paper tremendously if not restrained during the drying process.

Calligraphy on handmade paper by Molly McCright age 11

CALLIGRAPHY: And Another Natural Connection

Calligraphy relates to many artistic areas, such as painting, pottery, textile design, and book arts. Calligraphy and papermaking are intimately related: paper is the surface on which calligraphy most commonly appears.

For beginners, especially children, a good alternative to ink and

Fruits and vegetables necklace: handmade paper using ceramic techniques

The paper was cast in molds. When dry, holes were made using an electric drill and then the "paper produce" was threaded on the string.

steel nib pens are the relatively inexpensive ZIG markers, which are made in a variety of colors and are available in several nib sizes. Teaching calligraphy with ZIG markers makes classroom setup a breeze. Markers eliminate the inevitable ink spills and the blob of ink which always waits to fall until the last letter on the page.

Karen Charatan's book, *ABC Zig Calligraphy*, is full of wonderful, creative examples of calligraphy done by various well–known calligraphers from across the country, and provides inspiration as well as instruction.

Advanced students find endless possibilities when they begin making their own paper for writing. Many variations in making the sheet of paper can be tried to create a variety of writing surfaces. Generally, more highly beaten pulp, if it can be restrained when drying, makes paper with a smoother surface. Smoother felts also help make smoother paper. When paper is dried on flat surfaces, such as a board, the finished paper surface is smooth. External sizing helps close the surface of the paper to foster smoothness. Perhaps students could experiment with mixing Kaolin clay into their pulp as a filler to increase the opacity of the paper. Creating just the right paper for students' needs poses an exciting challenge for them.

After practicing calligraphy, projects can range from writing a poem on handmade paper, addressing a handmade paper envelope, creating a card or book from handmade paper, or simply writing students' names on handmade paper.

CERAMICS: Comparing Plastic Mediums

Clay and pulp share many significant similarities and have one great difference. Both are plastic mediums which can be molded into three–dimensional shapes, that when dry, will retain the molded form.

Clay and pulp also stick together from surface tension (scientists call it the Campbell effect, named after Boyd Campbell, the scientist who figured out what was going on). Surface tension draws fibers or particles together as water evaporates. Smaller particles, as in porcelain, or smaller fibers, as in highly beaten pulp, are drawn together more strongly than larger particles, creating more shrinkage. Just as papermakers use lightly beaten pulp for casting, a ceramic artist uses coarser clay for large work in which uneven shrinkage can be disastrous.

The big difference between clay and pulp is that when dry, clay is very heavy and pulp (paper) is very light.

Two possibilities for integrating these mediums are offered below. One involves applying ceramic techniques to papermaking. The other combines paper and clay to make mixed media art work.

Papermaking with Ceramic Techniques • Plaster molds from past projects can usually be found in any ceramics classroom. Use an existing plaster mold or make your own and cast it first in clay and then in paper. Compare the two objects and notice the differences. Decide which medium works best for expressing your ideas. Try using the some of the many tools for texturing clay to texture paper.

Mixed Media • Try a project where you incorporate both paper and clay. Challenge students to develop their own ideas or suggest something specific to create, such as jewelry. For example, beads can be made from both paper and clay and then combined to make earrings or a necklace. To keep the holes from closing due to shrinkage that occurs during the drying process, mold them around toothpicks or wooden skewers. *Do not remove the toothpicks or skewers until the paper is dry!* Since students need to consider the differing weights of both media to determine how paper and clay fit together, a unique engineering problem–solving opportunity is also created!

If you are setting up a space for papermaking in a high school, where there is often a ceramics room, clay and paper are quite compatible. Both need waterproof areas; clay in the pulp won't hurt anything, and even a little pulp in the clay shouldn't cause too many problems.

FIBER ARTS: A Close Relationship

The close relationship between paper and fabric begins with their source: fibers. Because of their similarity, projects which traditionally use fabric as a medium can often be translated into paper.

Weaving • A cloth called Shifu (*shi* means paper, *fu* means cloth) has been made and worn in Japan since the early 1600's. Thin strips of paper are cut and twisted to form threads, which are woven together

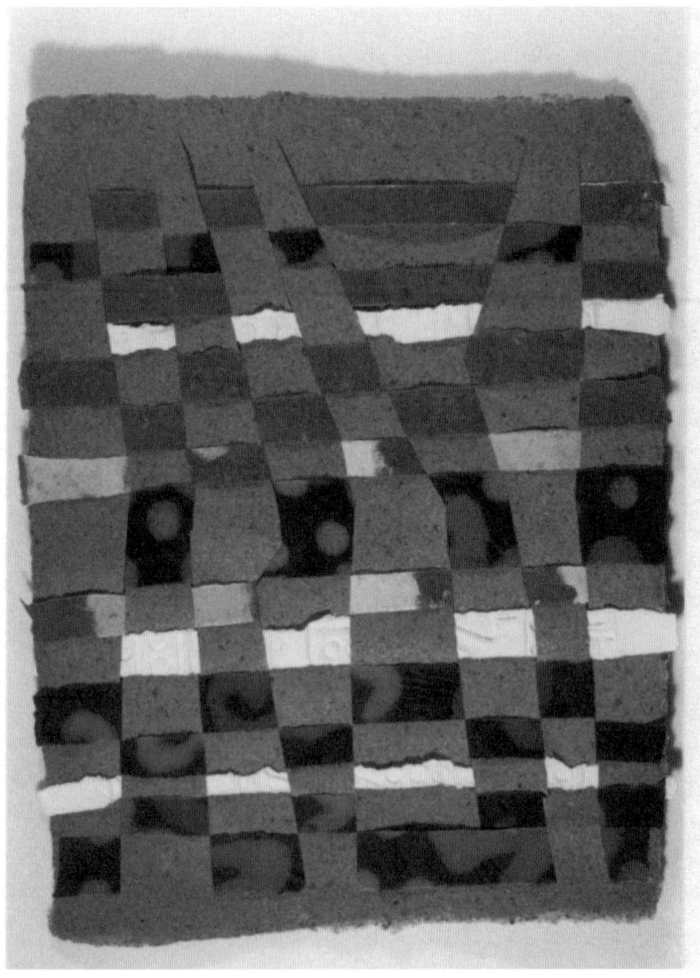

Weaving created from multiple sheets of handmade paper

to form the cloth. My friend, Neal Bonham, pointed out the interesting fact that as Europeans were making their paper from cloth, the Japanese were making cloth from paper!

While the *shifu* process is more complicated than an elementary classroom would allow, paper could certainly be integrated into a weaving project, such as the classic paper weaving every elementary school student is obligated to do. This project could easily be done with each student using two sheets of their own same–sized handmade paper.

On one piece of paper, cut lines spaced about one inch apart, starting approximately two inches from the top and ending two inches from the bottom, to create the *warp* for your weaving. On the other piece of paper, create the *weft* by cutting or tearing it into strips the opposite way from which you cut the warp.

Exchanging wefts with other students' paper introduces different colors into the weavings, and teaches cooperation and collaboration. The combined pieces using handmade paper are far richer than pieces done with construction paper.

Options:

- weaving paper warp with a cotton or woolen weft;
- weave paper AND fabric weft into a piece.

Information for older students learning the shifu technique can be found in the book *The Art and Craft of Papermaking* by Sophie Dawson. (See Bibliography.)

Surface Design • Two surface design techniques are *orizomegami* and *suminagashi*. Other decorated paper techniques include paste papers, batik, and stencil papers. For more information, see *A Guide to Making Decorated Papers* by Anne Chambers, or *Decorative Paper* by Diane Maurer–Mathison. Many of the surface design techniques used on fabric can also be applied to paper.

ORIZOMEGAMI is the Japanese art of folding and dyeing paper. Color is added to the paper using ink and or dye. Success with this technique depends on the paper used. The paper must be very absorbent and yet maintain strength while wet.

My favorite kind of handmade paper to use for orizomegami is made from kozo, a Japanese fiber. A machine–made paper called "Tableau Rice Paper," which I find in art supply stores, works well for classroom use, but don't hesitate to experiment with any type. Some handmade papers, especially recycled papers, may not be sufficiently strong or thin, but anything is worth a try.

Although an infinite number of folding patterns are possible, one possibility is to fan–fold the paper lengthwise. Then fan–fold the pleated bundle in the opposite direction, resulting in a small rectangular bundle of paper. (Consult *Decorative Paper* by Diane Maurer–Mathison for folding diagrams.) Next, after the paper is folded, dip it in water to wet it thoroughly. Press out the excess water by placing it between two wooden blocks and squeezing.

Next, dip the edges of the paper into the ink or apply ink to the edges with a medicine dropper. Use at least two different colors. Squeeze the paper between the blocks again if you want to create more bleeding. Unfold and let dry.

SUMINAGASHI is a Japanese marbling technique where inks are floated on water, and silk or paper are placed on the water's surface to

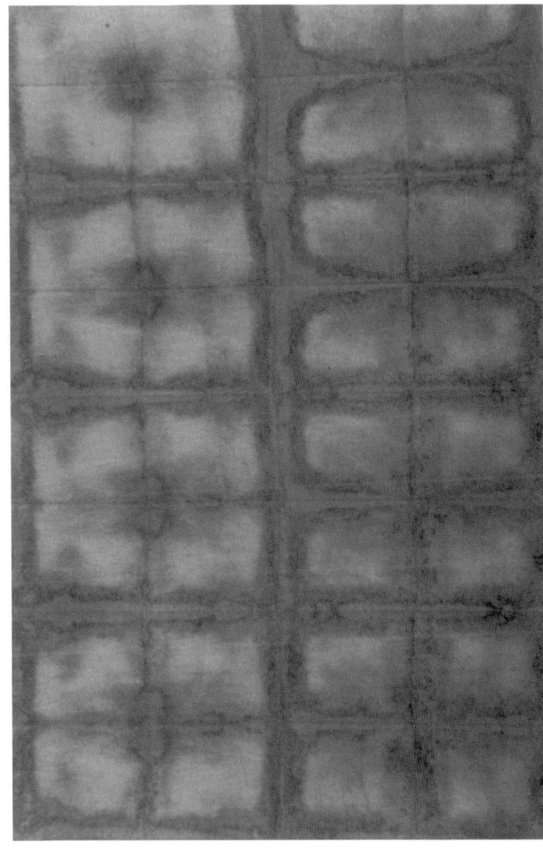

Orizomegami surface design technique on kozo paper

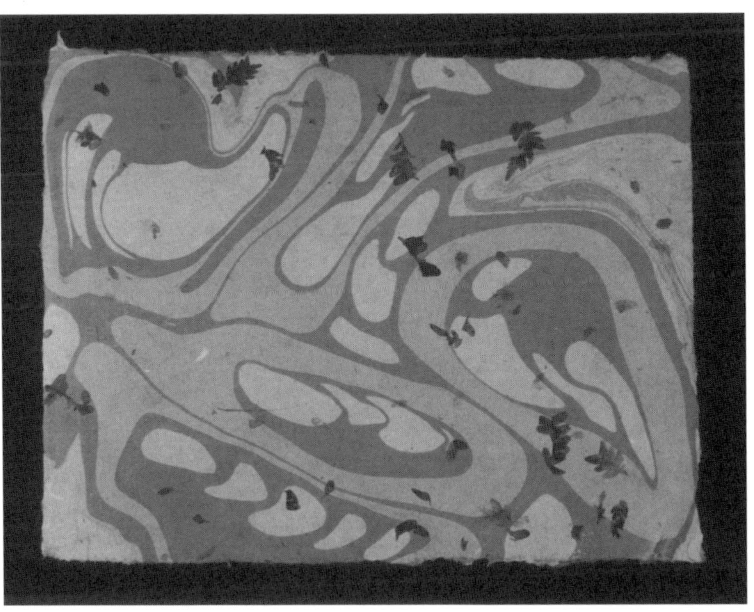

Suminagashi technique on handmade paper

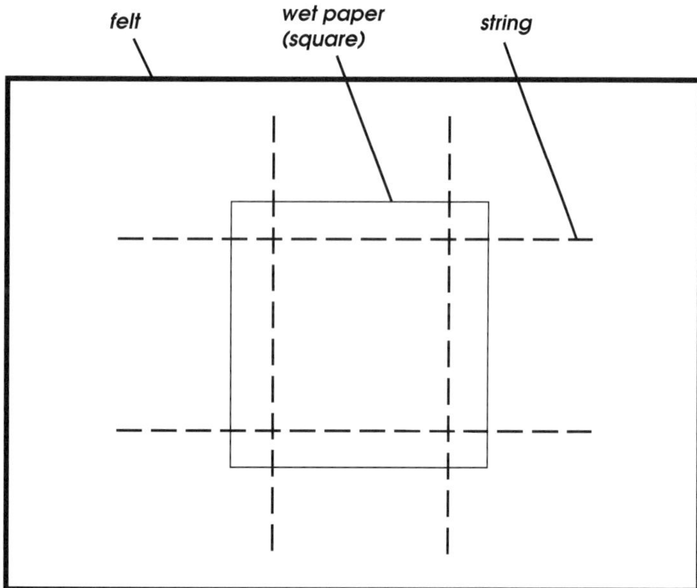

Figure 1

Embed strings for quilting in two ways:
1) dip strings in pulp and lay them on wet paper; or
2) lay strings in place on wet paper and laminate another sheet on top

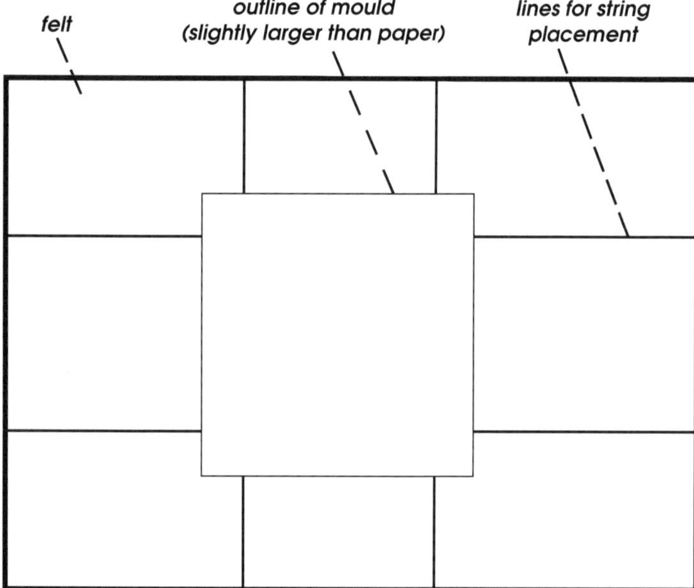

Figure 2

To maintain uniform size for paper squares and for placement of strings, trace outline of mould on felt with permanent marker and mark locations of strings on edge of felt

capture the resulting pattern. It's a fun and very magical process. For complete information on suminagashi marbling, consult Don Guyot's book, *Suminagashi: An Introduction to Japanese Marbling*, and a section from Diane Maurer's book, *Marbling*. Prepared inks can be used for both suminagashi and orizomegami. However, with older students or with small groups of younger children, an informative process would be to purchase ink sticks and have them grind their own ink.

Stitching • Paper may be stitched by hand or on a machine. Recycled paper is not the best to use for stitching because of its weakness. Papers made from a fiber such as abaca hold up quite well.

Basketry • A variety of techniques can be used to make baskets and other vessels out of paper. The most commonly used technique is casting. *Papermaking for Basketry*, edited by Lynn Stearns, is entirely devoted to this topic. Each chapter highlights an artist who makes baskets using handmade paper. The book describes their techniques, has many photographs of their work, and is an excellent source of inspiration for students.

Quilts • Paper can be used in a variety of ways to create a "quilt." Quilts make excellent group projects in classroom settings. For a quilt, students each make their own squares. A theme can be chosen, such as "the environment," and each student can design a quilt square relating to this theme. The quilt can be assembled in one of several ways:

1) Glue the squares to a piece of paper or foamcore board.
2) Stitch the squares by hand or by machine to a piece of paper or cloth. The cloth could be stretched on a frame for hanging or for framing and hanging.
3) Embed four strings in each square as it is made. (*See diagrams at left.*) Tie the strings together to connect the quilt.

To make the squares for the third method of assembly mentioned above, first, pull and couch a square sheet of paper. Then, lay down the four strings on this sheet of paper. (*See Figure 1.*) Next, form another square sheet and laminate it on top of the first square, embedding the strings between the two sheets of paper. Since the threads must be an equal distance from the edges of the paper, put marks on the felts so students are able to laminate their sheets directly on top of each other; otherwise, the sheets will be a variety of sizes and the threads will not line up when tying the squares together. (*See Figure 2.*) Caution students to center the strings so they are long enough on each end to tie them together.

An alternate way to embed strings onto the paper is by dipping the tautly held strings into the pulp and then laying them on the paper square. Using this method, a second sheet of paper is not needed. Finally, add imagery to square. When the paper is dry, tie the squares together to form the quilt.

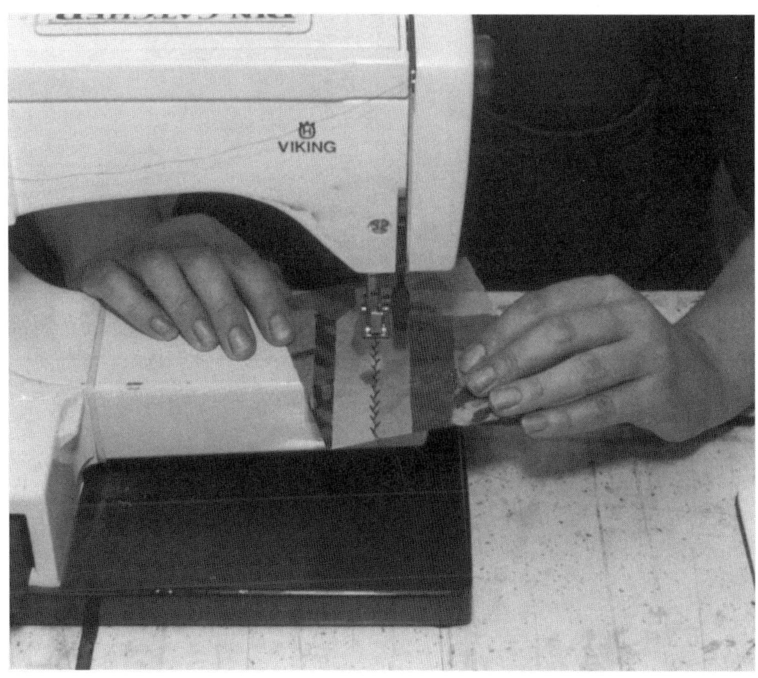

Stitching paper on sewing machine

Finished quilt square of handmade paper

"Bird"
by
Brandon Hysell
age 10

PHOTOGRAPHY: Printing on Handmade Paper

Photographic prints can be made on handmade paper by coating the paper with emulsions (blueprinting, brownprinting, silver nitrate, and the like). Be aware that the chemicals used for these processes are poisonous.

Work only in well–ventilated areas, wear gloves, purchase pre–mixed solutions, clean all spills immediately and dispose of all wastes properly. Because such precautions are necessary, I recommend these techniques only for high school students in advanced classes. Since its process is very toxic, avoid blueprinting with children.

For more information, ideas, and pictures of examples, I highly recommend the book *The New Photography* by Catharine Reeve and Marilyn Sward. For anyone teaching or doing their own photography, *The New Photography* is an excellent resource. Another good source of information is the article "Photo/Paper: Five Easy Processes" by Marilyn Sward, published in *Hand Papermaking*, Vol. 6, No. 1, Summer 1991. Since my knowledge of the art of photography is very limited, the following information is adapted from their book.

Consider the following information when making paper for printing with emulsions.

- In order to accept emulsions and safely survive the photographic chemical processes, handmade paper must be strong enough to withstand soaking in water for 15 minutes. If it buckles excessively or becomes so soft that the fibers begin to separate, the paper is not satisfactory.
- Sizing will help make your paper strong enough for photographic processes. With the addition of sizing, paper becomes water–resistant. The amount and type of sizing determines the paper's strength and water–resistance, as well as whether the paper is limp or stiff.

Paper can be sized internally or externally. Internal sizing is added to the pulp before the paper is made. External sizing is applied after the paper has been formed and dried. Both methods work. Internal sizing allows the surface character of the paper to remain visible and is easier to manage, since the sizing material is mixed into the pulp after beating. However, internal sizing may not always be enough to prevent emulsion from staining into inner layers of fiber.

While a variety of paper sizings are available, probably the best sizing for adapting handmade papers to photographic use is Hercon internal sizing, which can be obtained from papermaking suppliers. To size paper, add 1/4 cup of sizing per pound of dry weight of fiber at the end of the beating cycle. Or add 1 teaspoon of sizing per 1 cup of pre–soaked linter pieces when processing paper pulp in a blender. Hercon, an alkylketene dimer, becomes effective in the paper after several days or with added heat, which an iron or hair dryer can provide. Gelatin sizing or spray starch are examples of other sizings which can be used for some photo processes.

- Titanium dioxide, which brightens your sheet, can be added to the pulp at a rate of 3 grams for every 100 grams of dry fiber.
- When forming sheets of paper, be sure to make a few extra that you can cut up and use for photographic test strips.

To use your paper for photographic prints after it is formed, coat a sheet with emulsion, using one of the following methods: 1) brush the emulsion onto the paper with a bristle brush, a foam brush, a blanchard brush, a Japanese brush or a fan brush; 2) use rubber gloves to fingerpaint the emulsion onto your paper; 3) rub it on with a sponge; or 4) float the paper on the emulsion. Different methods create different effects. Take care not to get too much emulsion on your paper. Good instructions are included with Liquid Light.

Self–portrait by Amy Bassett, grade 9 computer graphics student

First, a positive/negative portrait was created on computer. Then, a stencil was cut from portrait and used to make image from pulp.

COMPUTER GRAPHICS: Hand–Made / Machine–Made

Handmade paper can run through most computer printers. Students should practice making sheets for a time before attempting to put their paper through a printer, since unevenly formed sheets can throw the printer out of whack. I have successfully printed on handmade paper with my dot matrix printer, with a laser printer and on an ink jet printer.

Experiment with unsized and sized papers to see which prints best. Comparing the results of printing the same image on machine–made paper and handmade paper is a good activity for heightening awareness and sensitivity. Explore the concept of the contrast in printing with a machine on handmade paper versus machine–made paper.

Create drawings with the computer and translate them into handmade paper by making a stencil from the drawing. Or use the drawing as a study for translation into a pulp painting.

Sculpture:
Origami dragonflies attached to paper tile collage, creating a three-dimensional wall piece

"Safe Haven: Dragonflies" by the author

SCULPTURE: A Strong, Yet Lightweight, Medium

Paper can be used in sculpture in two ways: using paper as one of the mediums in a mixed media piece, or by using the paper itself as the medium. When paper is used as the medium, it can either be cast (see "Casting," page 52) or the sheets can be used alone.

By folding and cutting sheets of paper in various ways, three-dimensional objects can be created. Origami is one familiar example. Related methods include paper sculpture and pop-up book structures.

Many books explaining these methods are available, including *The Encyclopedia of Origami and Papercraft Technique* by Paul Jackson, *Paper as Art and Craft: The Complete Book of the History and Process of the Paper Art* by Newman, Newman and Newman, *The World of Origami* by Isao Honda, and *How to Make Super Pop-Ups* by Joan Irvine.

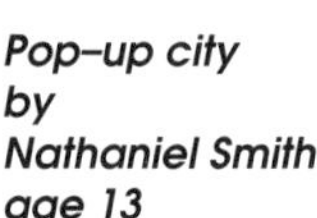

Pop-up city by Nathaniel Smith age 13

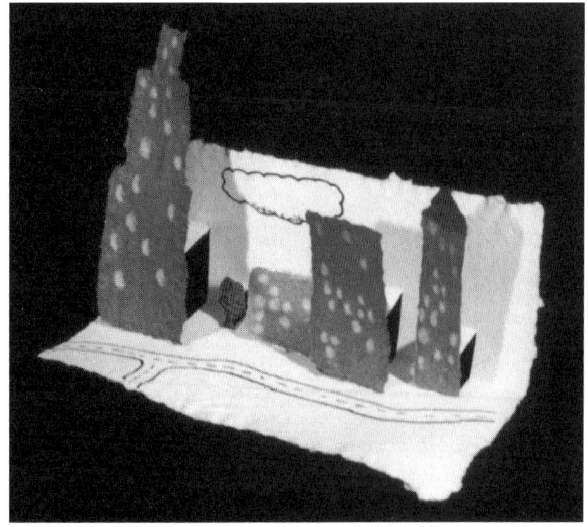

PERFORMING ARTS: Masks, Costumes and Scenery

Precedence has been established for artists to design sets and costumes for the theater. Examples include glass artist Dale Chilhuly's set for The Seattle Opera's 1993 production of Debussy's "Pelleas and Melisande" and Maurice Sendak's set designs for the opera version of his book *Where the Wild Things Are*. Sendak also designed costumes and sets for a production of Mozart's "The Magic Flute" and for Janácek's "The Cunning Little Vixen."

Since paper is a lightweight and plastic medium, it makes an ideal material with which to create theatrical sets and costumes. A flame retardant can be purchased and brushed or sprayed onto a dry paper surface to reduce flammability. Paper can be made in any shape, size or thickness. Masks can be made using the techniques described in Chapter Four. (See "Casting," page 52.)

Pulp spraying, although not discussed here, is a technique appropriate to large items, such as scenery and backdrops, and is suitable for high school level and above. Find more information on pulp spraying technique in *The Art and Craft of Papermaking* by Sophie Dawson.

Mask cast on styrofoam base by Laurel Smith, age 12

INDUSTRIAL ARTS: Making Tools

One way of inexpensively obtaining the tools you need for papermaking is by enlisting the aid of the industrial arts teacher and classes.

Suggest a project to make a simple press like the one described in Arnold Grummer's book, *Paper by Kids*. Because a hydraulic jack is used with this press, a science lesson could be integrated by teaching the students about hydraulics. See Chapter Seven, page 103.

Make moulds and deckles as another project. The level of sophistication of the moulds and deckles could vary, depending on the skill levels of the students involved. Frames for simple vats could also be constructed.

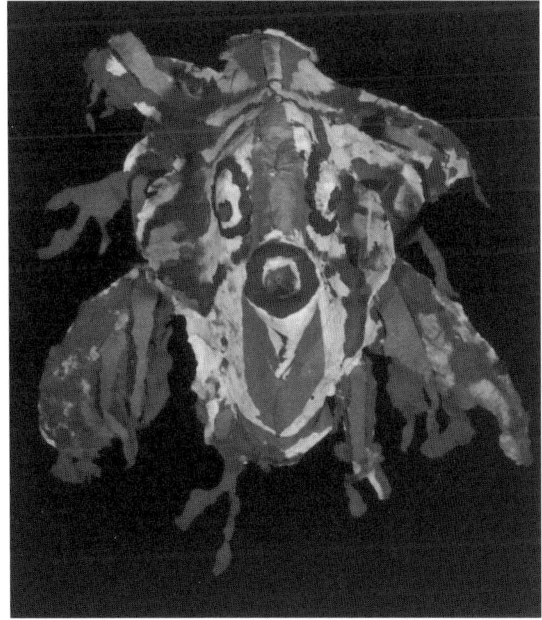

Fish mask created by casting pulp on a clay base covered with Saran Wrap™

Craftsmanship: origami box

THE ART OF LIVING: Craftsmanship and Following Directions

Making the origami boxes described below can help reinforce the two important life skills of craftsmanship and following directions, which often are not emphasized at home or at school.

For young students, you will probably want to demonstrate how to make origami boxes. For older students, you might want to give them the written process described below, along with the diagrams, offering them practice at reading and following directions on their own.

Craftsmanship is very important in creating these boxes. Accuracy and care in their construction makes a world of difference in the quality of the finished product. See Appendix for reproducible sheets of the diagrams and directions.

Directions for Making Origami Boxes

1. Cut two squares of paper. One square must be 1/4–inch larger than the other. ACCURACY IS IMPORTANT!
2. Starting at opposite corners of the paper, mark diagonal lines with a pencil.
3. Fold corners to the center "X".
4. Fold two opposite sides to the center point. Unfold.
5. Fold the other two opposite sides to the center. Unfold.
6. Cut on the fold lines on two opposite edges. You will have two cuts on opposite edges (4 total cuts).
7. On the sides where you have cut, pull out the two opposite sides. Fold up the sides that have not been pulled out to form a box.
8. Bring the pulled–out side over the folded–up sides and glue down on the inside, if necessary.
9. Repeat steps 2 through 8 for the other square.
10. If folded accurately, the larger square will fit neatly over the smaller square to form a wonderful covered box!

Related Activity: *Language Arts* • *Storytelling*

The making of another type of origami box can be taught by telling the story "The Brothers Short and The Brothers Long," found in *The Family Storytelling Handbook* by Anne Pellowski. Instructions are included for folding the box while telling the story.

Making ORIGAMI BOXES

FOLD LINE
PENCIL LINE
CUT

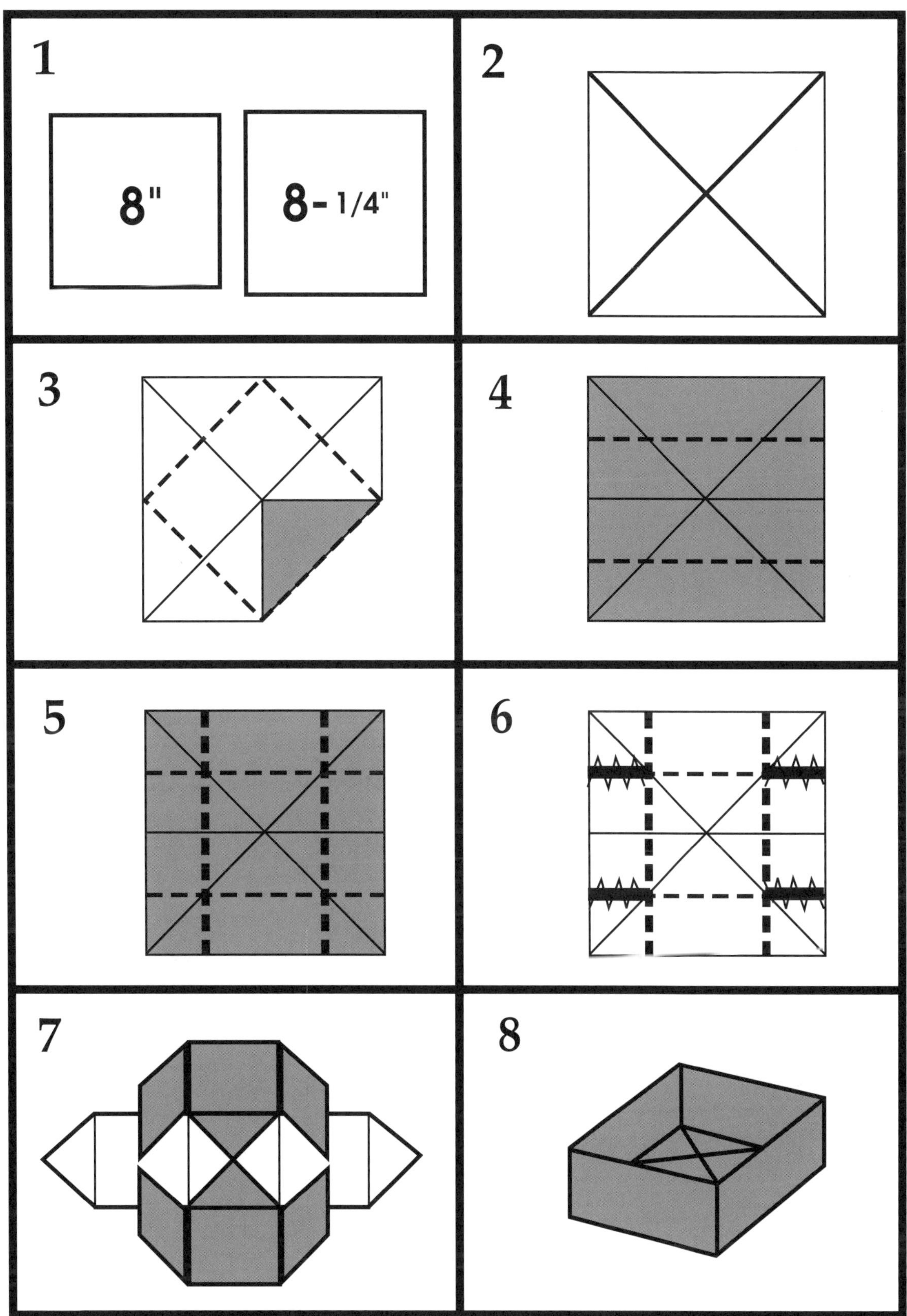

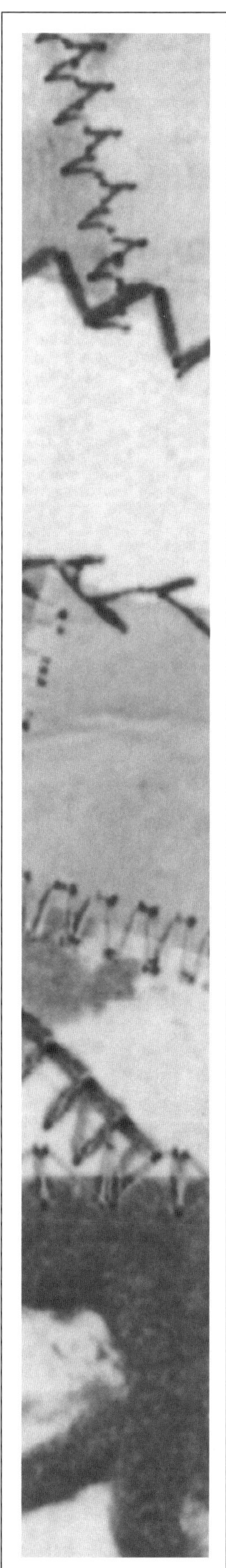

Chapter Seven

Integrating Papermaking with Basic Curriculum

In today's schools, integrating curricula is considered highly desirable. Descriptive words for the variety of models include *connected, nested, sequenced, shared, webbed, threaded, integrated, immersed* and *networked*. No doubt other adjectives apply, as well. Few teachers would argue against organizing the curriculum in this manner. I remember my many classes of art history. In the most exciting ones, the instructor taught about the art, the history, the philosophy, and the literature of the time period.

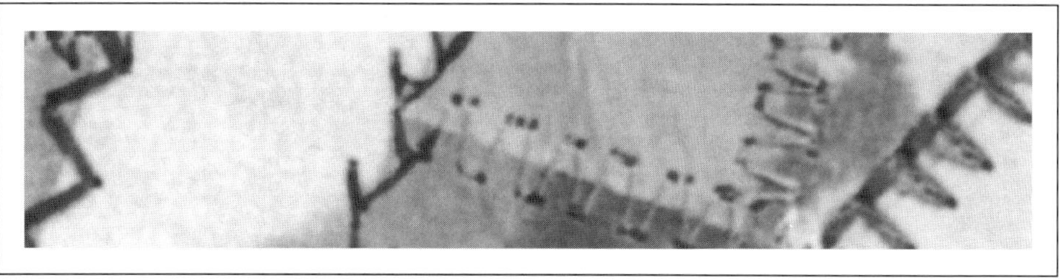

Today, however, many teachers surely wonder how to find the time — between attending meetings, monitoring the halls, supervising recess and lunch, grading papers and holding conferences — to plan an integrated curriculum, let alone teach it. With the materials in this book, I hope individual teachers find the integrating of content with disciplines an easier task to perform, and that teachers are encouraged to collaborate on the shared teaching of similar content.

LANGUAGE ARTS: Spelling/ Vocabulary

Papermaking, like any other craft, has its own vocabulary. Select words from the following list for students to learn, define, and spell.

pulp
: plant fibers used for papermaking that have been cooked and beaten and are ready to be formed into sheets of paper

vat
: container used to hold pulp and water for dipping the mould and deckle, forming a sheet of paper

mould or mold
: rigid frame covered with a screen on which pulp is pulled from the vat

deckle
: a rigid frame that rests on the surface of a mould while a sheet of paper is being formed; prevents paper pulp from overflowing the mould; gives paper a feathered edge, characteristic of handmade paper

couching (kooching)
: transferring the sheet of paper from the mould to the felt

watermark
: lighter marks made on paper by various wires attached to the mould, often in special designs

papyrus
: writing surface formed by laying slices of the papyrus stalk at right angles to each other and pounding with a mallet to bind them into "paper;" not true paper because the plant is not separated into tiny fibers, but one of the oldest writing surfaces similar to paper

felt
: cloth on which the wet sheets are placed during the couching process

cellulose
: substance derived from plants to make paper

Hollander beater
: traditional piece of equipment used in Western–style papermaking for beating fibers prior to sheetforming

sizing
: water–resistant materials added to paper in its pulp stage or after drying; makes paper more water–resistant

pigment
: finely ground coloring material added to pulp to make colored paper

emboss
: to impart a design or pattern in the paper surface; achieved by pressing paper against a three–dimensional object

post
: a stack of wet–formed paper sheets alternated with felts; placed in the press to remove excess water

LANGUAGE ARTS: Writing In Sequence

Before teaching the papermaking process, let students know that they will be asked to tell you about or write about how paper is made.

The basic steps in papermaking are:

1) gather fiber
2) soak fiber
3) cook fiber
4) beat fiber
5) color fiber (optional)
6) form sheets using a mould and deckle
7) couch the paper onto a felt (turn over the mould with the fibers on it onto the fabric)
8) press the paper
9) dry the paper

This exercise can be used with very young students if you write each step on a card and ask them to put the cards in proper order. (See Appendix for a page to make reproducible cards.) Older students should be able to list the steps.

Advanced students can write an expository paragraph detailing the steps involved in papermaking. Provide a list of transitional words and phrases such as *and, and then, then, next, first, secondly, thirdly, finally, last, lastly, immediately, soon, in the meantime, afterward*. Ask students to use some of these words in their writing. Or challenge your students by asking them to write a process analysis paragraph, where they detail not only what steps should be taken, but also explain why those steps are needed.

LANGUAGE ARTS: Creative Writing

Paper is everywhere in our lives. From the minute we get up in the morning, we start using paper. *Assignment*: Write what your day would be like without paper.

To help students get started, you might have them first list all the activities they take part in during a day, which should give them a new awareness. We do so much habitually, without really thinking about it. To take this activity one step further, ask students to think of some new uses for paper, and/or some inventions using paper.

Below and to the right are some responses to this assignment, from papers written by students in Ms. Timm's fifth grade class at Pierce Elementary School in Cedar Rapids, Iowa in March 1994.

- ***"When you watch t.v. you usually don't remember or think about the actors having to use paper scripts to memorize their lines."***
— Becky Hanson

- ***"I think there would be some problems. Like sports cards will be made of stone or a metal, which would drive the cost of cards up. Maps would be harder to fold and they would weigh a ton."***
— Ben Armfield

- ***"If you think about it, the world would be no fun without it. For instance, that big paper airplane that you flew in class when the teacher wasn't looking. Or that imaginary submarine out of a cardboard box. Dad reading the funnies, and you reading your birthday invitation, the party of the year. There will be confetti and everything."***
— Melinda Cote

- ***"If there was no paper in the world life would be boring. You couldn't keep anything in school except clay crafts you make in art. There would be no reason to have typewriters and computers because you wouldn't be able to type or print anything. You could only watch or listen to the news because there wouldn't be a newspaper. You couldn't even have a phone book to look up phone numbers and you would have to remember everything by heart. You couldn't send people letters. There wouldn't be books to study from so you would have a hard time getting 100% on your tests. Without paper, origami can't be done and it is a really fun thing to do."***
— Jason Johnson

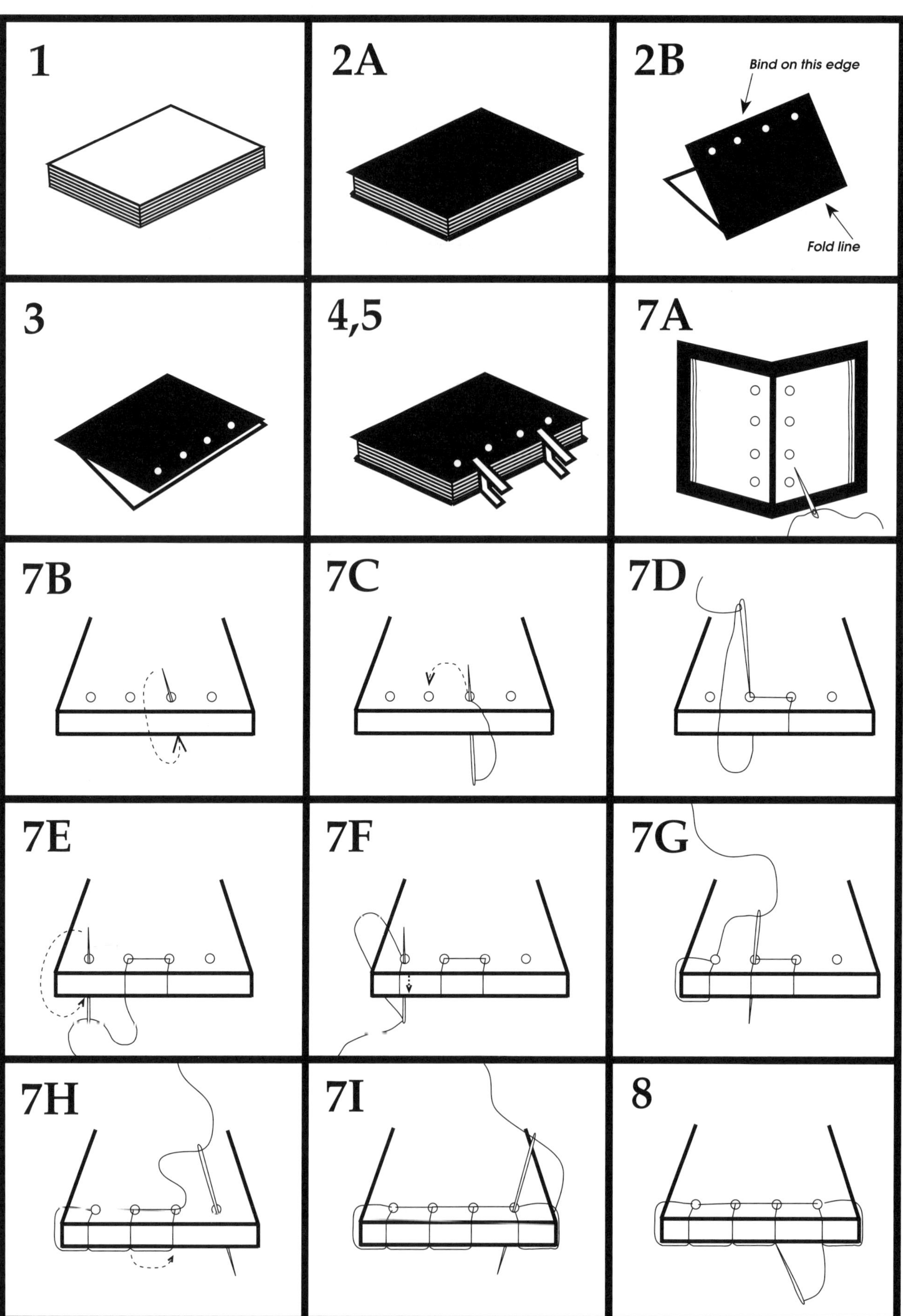
1
2A
2B
Bind on this edge
Fold line
3
4,5
7A
7B
7C
7D
7E
7F
7G
7H
7I
8

LANGUAGE ARTS: Making a Book

Binding a book can be done several ways. A very simple Japanese bookbinding technique is described below. For further details, consult one of the books listed in the bibliography.

Much pleasure can be derived from binding your writings into a book. Creating such a book can build esteem in students and help them think of themselves as authors rather than merely students. In terms of a craft, the book has become an art form in itself, offering many creative possibilities for bookmaking. A separate discipline, called "Book Arts," concerns itself with making finely crafted and aesthetically pleasing books, which are themselves works of art.

Bookbinding Process • See Appendix for reproducible diagrams and directions.

Tools Needed:

Paper for pages and cover
Pencil
Ruler
Awl
Cotton warp thread (or similar)
Needle (blunt end with eye large enough to thread)

1) Neatly pile the sheets of your text in a stack.
2) Place one cover sheet on top and one cover sheet on the bottom. The cover is often slightly larger and chosen from a heavier weight paper than the paper which is used for the text. If you are using the same weight of paper for the cover as for the text, make it heavier by using a sheet which is twice as big and folding it in half, with the fold being the outer edge and opposite the side where you bind.
3) Use a pencil to lightly mark the cover with the locations where holes are to be punched. Four is a traditional number of holes, but any number will work.
4) Position the pages between the two covers. Keep the pages from shifting by placing several clothespins along the edge of the book to be bound.
5) Punch the holes in the binding with an awl, ice pick or similar tool.
6) Select a thread and a needle for sewing your book. In Japan, silk and hemp are traditionally used. I often use a readily available cotton warp thread, but try any thread you have on hand. For decorative purposes, you can use more than one thread.
7) Begin to sew by starting at any hole on the spine of the book. Lift two or three sheets of the text. Insert the needle under these sheets and bring it up through the hole and out, leaving a short tail inside the book. Bring the needle around the spine to the front of the book and then up again through the same hole. Proceed to the next hole and continue, as shown in the drawings.
8) Continue stitching until you eventually return to the place where you started. Put the needle back through the same hole and bring it out between the two sheets of text where you began. Tie the thread with its tail and snip off the threads at the knot.

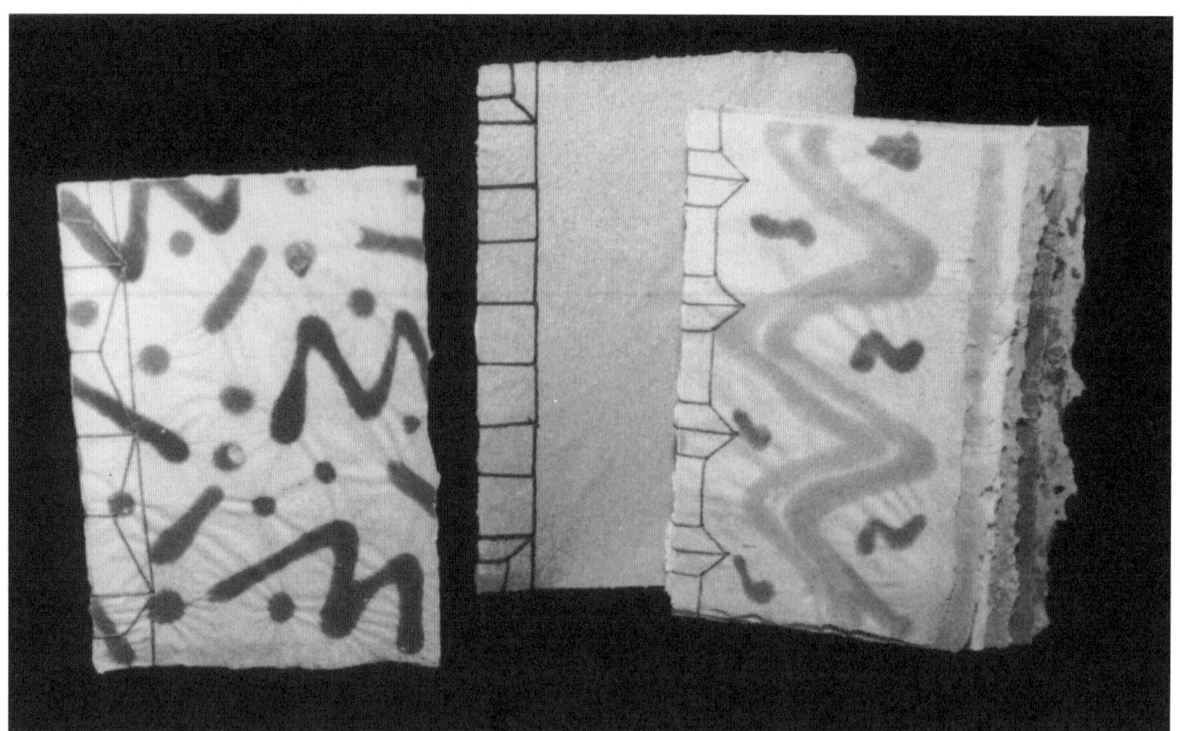

Variations of simple Japanese bookbinding techniques

L to R: hemp–leaf binding, noble binding, tortoise shell binding

drawing by papermaking residency student

Melissa Short grade 5

SCIENCE: Looking at Paper through a Microscope

Paper is not a solid like metal or plastic. Paper is made of many, many cellulose fibers and other fibers that come from plants.

Look at a piece of paper through a microscope to see the individual fibers which make up each sheet.

Try many different types of paper and notice the differences.

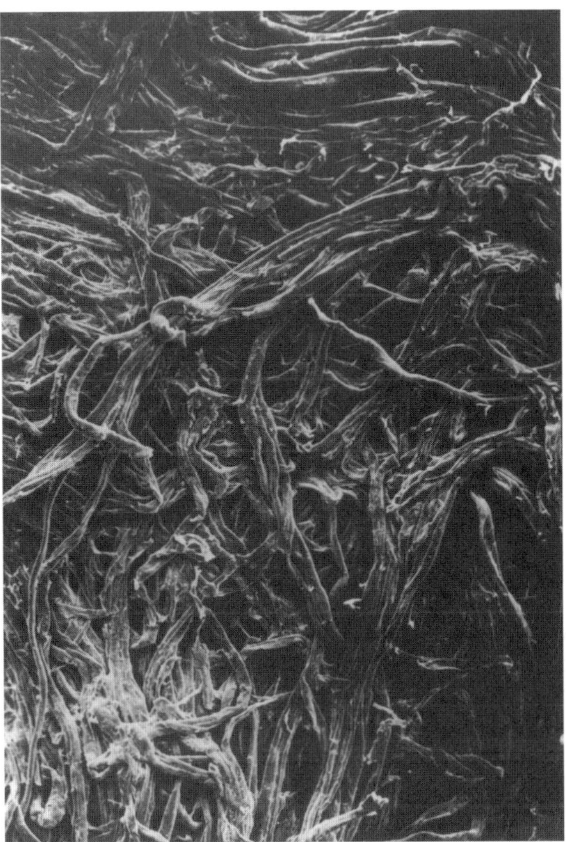

loose papermaking fibers, before beating

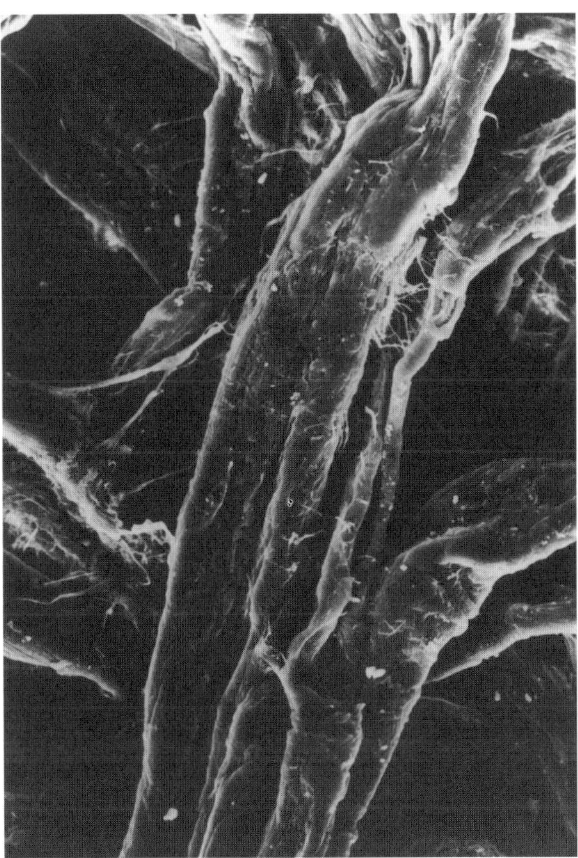

papermaking fibers showing "fibrils" raised from main fiber surface during beating

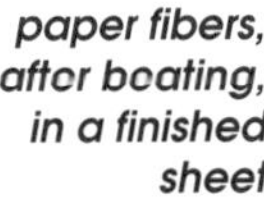

paper fibers, after beating, in a finished sheet

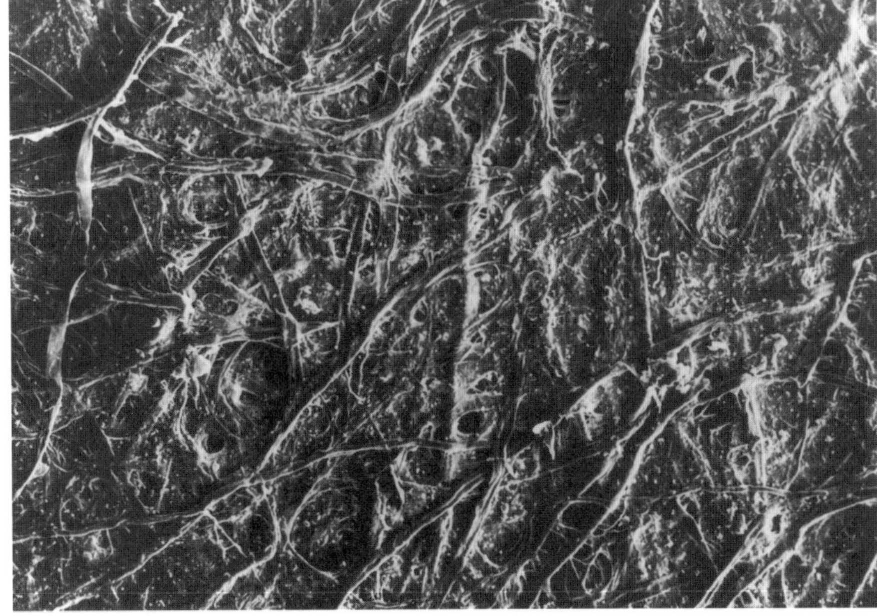

QUESTIONS and ANSWERS about The Science of Papermaking

by Timothy Barrett

Once children are engaged in the process of making paper, they often become curious about how and why it works. "Why do all those little pieces of plant fiber come together to form a sheet of paper?" "Why don't we have to mix in some paste in the water to make it hold together?" These are good questions, and well worth following up informally during papermaking, or more formally later, as an actual lesson and discussion about the more scientific aspects of papermaking.

Two responses are offered here: a very simple reply, perhaps best for very young children, and then, a more detailed, but still very basic, introduction to the topic. Those who would like to tackle the subject in a more comprehensive way are referred to W.R. Cowan's eleven–page pamphlet, *Why Paper is Paper*, which includes simple experiments that can be conducted in a classroom to prove the theory. Write to the Friends of Dard Hunter (see Appendix) to purchase a copy.

Question:

• How do fibers in water come together to make a piece of paper?

Answer #1:

First of all, it's important to remember that we must use cellulose fibers. We can't make paper out of animal fibers, like wool or hair, or from plastic or metal fibers. We have to use cellulose fibers, like cotton or wood. Next, the fibers must be beaten up in water. Beating makes the fiber a little shorter, but it also helps water get inside the fiber and stick to its surface. In general, cellulose fibers *like* water, and water *likes* cellulose. When you beat them and mix them up together a lot, they really *like* each other! Now, water doesn't seem sticky, but it really is, just a little. Because the water acts sticky on the surface of the fibers, it helps hold the fibers together in a damp sheet of paper after you make it. (If you don't think water is really helping hold fibers together, just try making a sheet of paper using dry fiber and no water. It's almost impossible to get the fibers to spread out into an even sheet, and what's worse, since the fibers are dry, they don't stick together at all!)

So why don't the fibers all fall apart when the sticky water goes away as the sheet dries? Ah! A very good question, and this is the secret of papermaking. After you make a sheet of paper and press it, and let it start to dry, the "sticky" water keeps the fibers together. And even though you can't see it happening, as the paper starts to dry, the water makes the fibers stick together closer and closer and closer. Until, guess what? The cellulose fibers get so close, they stick right to each other, tight! That's the magic of papermaking: cellulose fibers will stick to other cellulose fibers but not by themselves alone. They need water, and they need you to mix up the fibers in water, and they need you to make them into a sheet, with all that ever–so–slightly sticky water. Then, when no one is watching, when no one can see because the fibers are so tiny, the water sticks the fibers together so tight, the fibers stick to each other by themselves — and don't need the water any more! Paper!

Answer #2:

Cellulose fibers can be made into a strong piece of paper (without any glue or adhesive) because of an unusual and wonderful interaction that takes place between water and cellulose. To understand the big picture, it's first important to understand the two key components: water and cellulose. Let's start with water. H_2O, right? Two atoms of hydrogen and one of oxygen. Now, it so happens that when they're all together in a molecule of water, they don't line up in a row, they always end up looking like this *(see Figure 1)*:

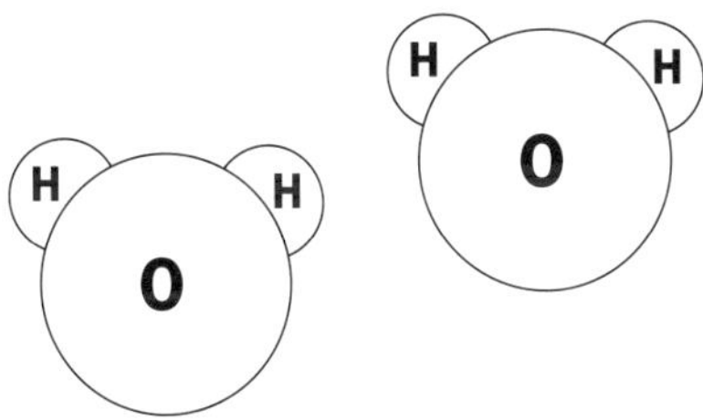

Figure 1

"Like Mickey Mouse," says my papermaker friend Howard Clark. This is always the case, and it has to do with the way the electrons and nuclei of the three atoms interact when they're together as a molecule of water. We wouldn't be too concerned about the Mickey Mouse configuration, except for one very important thing. It means a molecule of water is a *polar* molecule, which means that, much like a magnet is polar, a molecule of water has positive and negative ends. *(See Figure 2.)*

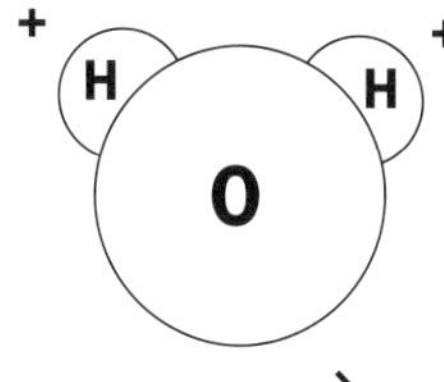

Figure 2

And molecules of water can attach to each other like magnets. The attachment is called a *hydrogen bond (see Figure 3)*. Now, you wouldn't think that's such a big deal, but it turns out to have very interesting effects. Hydrogen bonds explain why a water spider can walk on the surface of a pond without going under. In the water, under the surface, all the hydrogen bonds are irregular. But, at the boundary of the water and the air — at the surface of the pond — all the water molecules line up so tightly and the hydrogen bonds are so orderly that the water molecules actually form a kind of skin on the water surface where the insect can walk. Okay. Now, just remember this characteristic of water, because we'll come back to it in a minute.

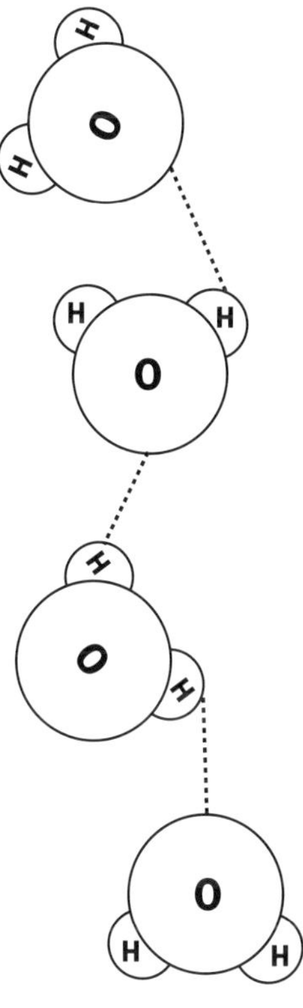

Figure 3

Let's shift to cellulose fibers for a second, and then, we'll put the water together with the cellulose and see how they interact to make paper.

Remember the polar nature of water molecules? The plus and minus sites? Well, it turns out that cellulose molecules have a similar characteristic. Except that cellulose molecules are very long (that's why fibers are so long — they're made up of billions and billions of long cellulose molecules). We're interested in the location on the cellulose molecule called a hydroxyl group. It's part of the cellulose molecule and it sticks up from the surface, like this *(see Figure 4)*:

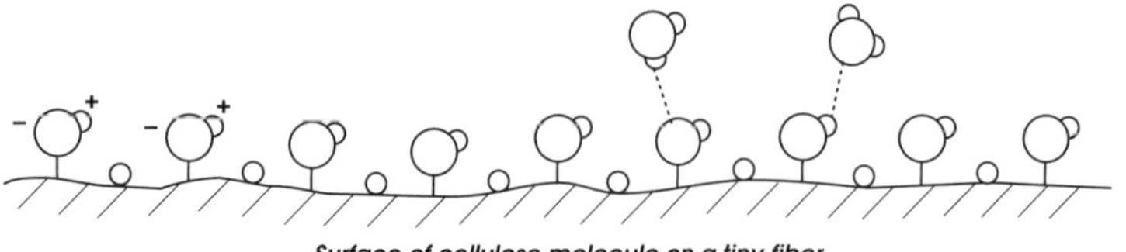

Figure 4

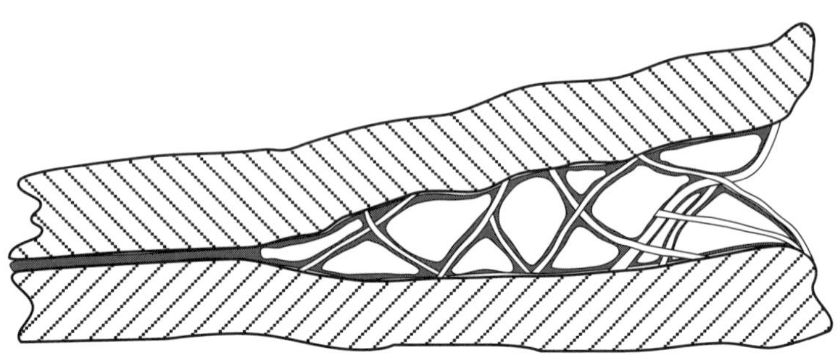

Figure 5
fibrils on cellulose surfaces during water removal

Source: James D'A. Clark. *Pulp Technology and Treatment for Paper.* Miller Freeman. 1978.

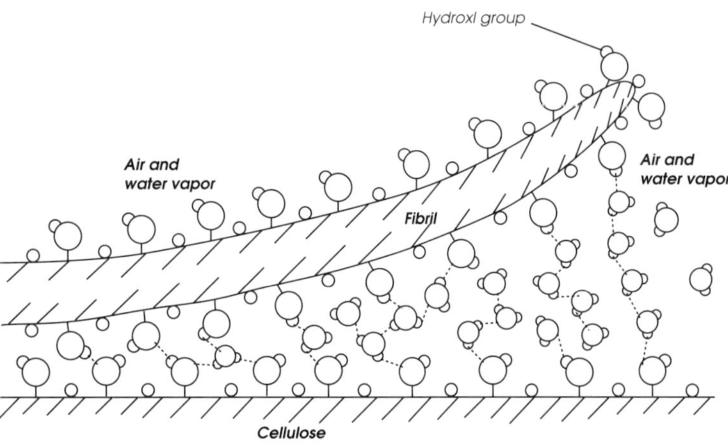

Figure 6
water molecules between two cellulose surfaces

Source: James D'A. Clark. *Pulp Technology and Treatment for Paper.* Miller Freeman. 1978.

See the plus and minus sites? Why do you think this might be important to the relationship between cellulose and water? Because water can form a hydrogen bond with a hydroxl group on the cellulose just as readily as it can with another molecule of water. Cellulose *likes* water, and the more we can do to increase the exposed hydroxyl groups on cellulose molecules, the more water attaches to it. This happens when we beat fiber before making sheets of paper, because beating helps open up the fibers, raise little tiny "fibrils" on their surfaces, and increase the exposed hydroxyl groups on cellulose molecules. The more we beat fiber, the more water attaches (and the slower the pulp drains when we make a sheet).

Now, let's put the two together, the cellulose and the water. After beating (which also helps shorten the fibers a bit, so they spread out more evenly), we mix the two together to make a sheet of paper. We press it and hang it up to dry. It sticks together. Why? There's no glue in between the fibers, just the water. If we could look very closely, we'd see, on a microscopic level, that water in between the fibers holds them together by forming hydrogen bonds *(see Figure 5)*.

As the paper dries, something very interesting begins to happen. Remember the "skin" on the surface of the pond where our spider friend could walk? This same skin, at the interface of the water and air in our sheet of paper, because it's so tight, actually *pulls* the fibers closer and closer together. Hydrogen bonds inside the water help, too. When only a few molecules of water are left as the paper dries, the pulling effect is so strong, it brings the fibers so close that, as the final molecules of water leave, hydrogen bonds form *between cellulose and cellulose! (See Figure 6.)*

This, plain and simple, is what makes paper so strong. The more you beat fiber before you form sheets, the stronger and crisper it gets, because you have created all those attachment places for water that can later become cellulose–to–cellulose bonding sites.

Question:

• If paper is made from such soft fibers, why can it cut you?

Answer:

It's true that fibers are soft at the start, but after they're beaten and made into paper, they bond together very tightly to make a tough, but still flexible, material. If you cut this material with a sharp knife, the edge of the paper will also be very sharp — and hard enough to cut you.

Question:

• If cellulose fibers are all pretty much the same, why are there so many different kinds of paper?

Answer:

First of all, there are really many different kinds of cellulose fiber. Cotton and wood fibers, for instance, are different from each other. Many different plants and trees have cellulose fiber that can be used for making paper, and they all make *different* kinds of paper. In addition, the way fiber is prepared is very important to the final type of paper. Different ways of cooking, bleaching and beating yield very different papers. Then, there are additives like dyes, pigments and clays that can change paper a lot. You can make the paper very thin or very thick. Finally, the way paper is dried and finished makes a big difference in its final surface.

SCIENCE: An Experiment in Beaten Fibers

Beating the fiber, which includes cutting, swelling, decurling, fibrillation, and fines production, is another critical aspect determining final paper quality. To understand beating, knowing the fiber's structure is helpful.

An informative experience for students would be to form sheets of paper using pulps which have been beaten for various lengths of time. The first sheet could be made from pulp beaten in the blender. The next pulp might be beaten for 45 minutes in a Hollander beater; the third, 1–1/2 hours; the fourth, four hours. Since its fiber changes dramatically with beating, abaca offers a good basis for demonstration. You can obtain the pulp if you know someone with a beater or by ordering the beaten pulp from a supplier.

Have students form, press and dry a sheet of paper from each vat of pulp. The sheets could be both air–dried and stack–dried. Ask them to write down their observations while they are forming sheets and again when they examine the dry sheets. Next, discuss their results and ask students to guess what caused the differences in each sheet. Students' final step is reading and research to find out what scientists and hand papermakers have learned about beating.

For more detailed information on beating, refer to W. F. Cowan's publication "Beating" in his *Science for Handpapermakers* series, available for sale by contacting the Friends of Dard Hunter.

SCIENCE and MATHEMATICS: Making Pulp From a Plant

Preparing pulp requires both math and science skills. Below are very general instructions for preparing plant fibers. Depending on the fiber you use, the amounts and times given will vary. Note that the measurements in the instructions are in *grams* and *liters*, providing students a chance to use the metric system. This is a great opportunity to teach an experimental approach. By trial and error, students could eventually determine the amount and times which produce the best results for the fiber being processed.

It *is* possible to pulp some plant fibers in a blender without cooking them. Gertrude Simon, who teaches papermaking residencies in South Carolina, suggests processing fresh marigolds in a blender to make a golden colored piece of paper. When I tried it, I found my hands turned gold, which made me think that this demonstration could also lead to a discussion on plant dyes.

Another fiber Simon processes without cooking is banana peels. She has students shred the peels into thin strings. Then they cut the strings with a scissors into small pieces and blend them. Simon advises it's helpful to add another fiber such as cotton or abaca, to improve bonding of the fibers. To process most fibers, you'll want to cook them first, using the guidelines below.

Directions:

1) Select a fiber. Some fibers are easier to process than others. If you are using a blender, you will want to avoid some plants which are all but impossible to process in the blender. Some fibers I have successfully processed with a blender are straw, corn, iris leaves and cattails.
2) Weigh the fiber. The dry weight should equal 750 grams (approximately 26 ounces). Cut the fiber into one– to two–inch lengths. With one person, the process seems to take forever, but with a classroom full of twenty–five scissors going at once, the fiber is ready in no time.
3) Soak the fiber for at least twelve (12) hours. Measure twelve (12) liters (approx. 3–1/6 gallons) of water into a stainless steel or enameled pot. In general, for each liter of water, use about 23 to 27 grams (between 3/4 and 1 ounce) of soda ash. Figure out how much soda ash is needed and measure out that amount. The exact amount will vary, depending on the type of fiber being processed.

- Keep accurate records for each batch of pulp, recording the amount of water and soda ash used, the dry weight of fiber, cooking time, and results, to determine whether increases or decreases in the amount of soda ash are needed. This is an opportunity for your students to practice developing charts and graphs.
- For a scientific approach, process different batches of pulp with different amounts of soda ash, so students can observe and record the differences. Soda ash can be purchased from swimming pool supply stores or papermaking suppliers.

4) Put the pot of water on a burner and bring it to a boil. When the water boils, add the soda ash, and then add the fiber. Start timing the "cooking" after bringing the water to a boil again. Boiling plant pulp has a distinct odor which many students may find offensive, so proper ventilation should be arranged.
5) Cooking usually takes approximately 2 to 4 hours, but fibers can be cooked 12 hours or more, if necessary. To test the fiber to see if it is sufficiently broken down, put a small amount with water in a blender and process it. When broken down, the fibers look somewhat like oatmeal. If the fiber doesn't break down, you will need to cook it longer.
6) After cooking, the fiber should be thoroughly rinsed and then finally beaten, by hand, by Hollander beater, or in a blender.

Consider the following two variables when cooking fiber: 1) the strength of the cooking solution (the ratio of soda ash to water) and 2) the amount of cooking time. A stronger solution takes less cooking time and a weaker solution takes more cooking time. Consider also the type of fiber and the method of beating. Some fibers are relatively easy to break down, while others are not. When using a blender for beating, fibers must be broken down more during the cooking process than when using a Hollander beater. Be aware that too strong a solution can destroy the fibers; too weak a solution will not fully cook the fibers.

Remember that these instructions are ***very, very*** general. Consult other papermaking books which go into more detail on preparing pulp, such as Lillian Bell's *Plant Fibers for Papermaking*, Timothy Barrett's *Japanese Papermaking*, or Sophie Dawson's *The Art and Craft of Papermaking*.

SCIENCE and MATHEMATICS: Hydraulics

Nothing so universally thrills young student papermakers as pressing the paper in the hydraulic press. One young student commented while watching me press the paper, "I had no idea that girls were so strong." While I considered telling him that the hydraulic jack was doing most of the work, I decided to leave him with his initial impression.

Using a hydraulic jack to press paper provides a perfect time to teach students the principles of hydraulics. Many science textbooks appropriate for middle school and older students contain information about hydraulics. Helpful diagrams can also be found in David Macaulay's *The Way Things Work*.

To operate a simple hydraulic jack, you first turn the release valve clockwise, which closes the oil valve. Next, you insert the handle in the pump and, by moving it up and down, you pump oil into a chamber underneath the big press piston. Each time you move the lever up and down, a small piston at the end of the handle does the pumping. If you look closely, you can see the small piston moving in and out as the handle goes up and down. The beauty of hydraulics is that the pressure you exert with the press handle on the little piston is multiplied by the same multiple (or ratio) of the difference in the sizes of the two pistons.

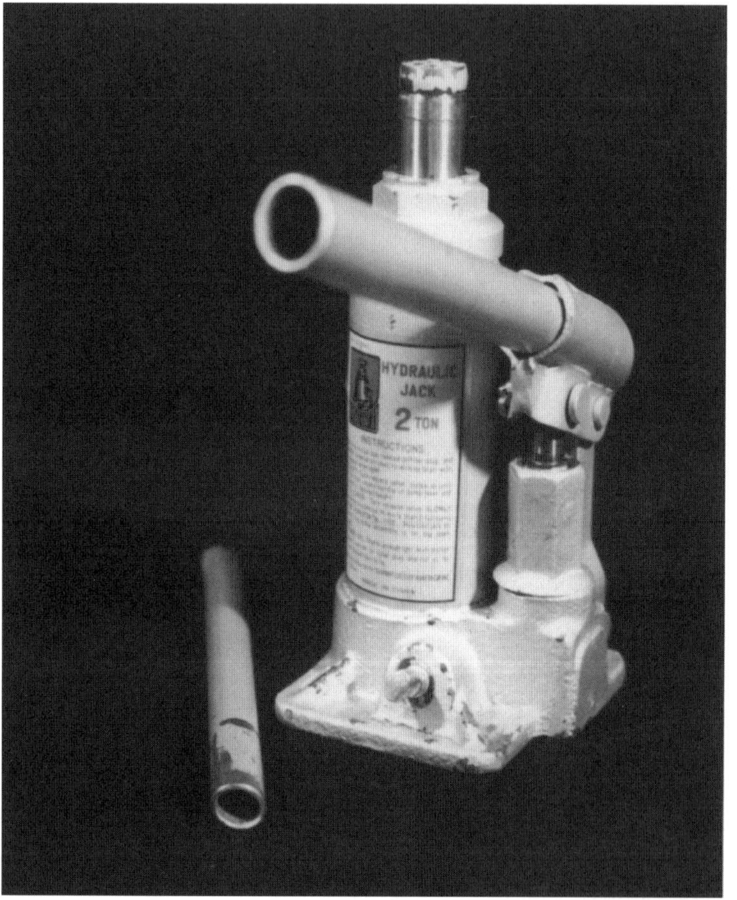

Basic hydraulic principles can be studied and demonstrated when pressing paper with a jack

For example, if the area of the little pump piston face is 1 square inch, and the area on the bottom of the main jack piston is 10 square inches, that's a ratio of 1:10. Then, if you generate 400 pounds of pressure on the oil, by pushing the handle down, the oil that pushes the big jack piston up is not 400, but 400 times 10, or **4000** pounds! Sounds like magic — and in a way, it is. The drawback is that the big jack piston goes up very slowly. You trade a lot a movement and a little pressure for a lot of pressure and little movement. Students will notice how the little pump piston moves up and down *a lot* compared to the tiny movements of the main jack piston.

To lower the piston, the oil valve is opened, removing pressure from the cylinder and allowing the piston to descend. Have students calculate how much they could lift if the little piston stayed the same, but the big jack piston had a diameter of about 32 inches, creating a piston face with area equal to 100 square inches. The new ratio is 1:100 (little piston size to big piston size). With this imaginary press, a child could lift 400 x 100 or 40,000 pounds — that's 16 cars stacked one on top of the other! But it would take a lot of pumping and the cars would only be lifted a few inches.

SCIENCE and MATHEMATICS: Pressure

The amount of pressure exerted on the paper while pressing determines how wet or dry the paper is when it comes out of the press. For students to know how much pressure they are applying to their paper when pressing, they need to understand the concept of *pounds per square inch (PSI).*

Two variables are involved in pressing paper. One is the amount of pressure used, and the other is the area (in square inches) on which the pressure is placed. When using a hydraulic jack , you can estimate the number of pounds of pressure being exerted. For example, if you are using a two–ton jack, you can estimate that you are exerting two tons of pressure. If you want to compare the amount of pressure a hydraulic jack can exert versus the amount of pressure a person can exert, you could use your students to demonstrate the concept.

On the floor, place a post of papers (either real or imaginary) sandwiched between two boards. Multiply the length times the width of the paper to determine the area of the paper in square inches.

Next, ask for student volunteers (ones who are not too shy to reveal their weight), and have one student stand on the board. The rest of the students can determine the amount of pressure being exerted on the paper by dividing the amount of pressure (student's weight in pounds) by the area of the paper (in square inches).

For example, papers which measure 14" x 20" have an area of 280 square inches. By dividing the area of the paper with the weight of a 120–pound student (120÷280), you find that the pressure exerted per square inch is approximately .43 PSI. To arrive at that figure, students must also use the mathematical skill of *rounding off.*

Now, ask another student to join the first. If the second student weighs 160 pounds, the students' combined weight is 280 pounds (280÷280), resulting in one (1) PSI, or one pound of pressure per square inch.

Another possibility is to have the same 120–pound student step onto a post of papers measuring 11" x 13". The resulting area is 143 square inches (120÷143), which gives .84 PSI or pounds of pressure per square inch.

Ask students to imagine that they could all stand on the post of papers. Have them estimate the total weight. For example, 24 students x 75 pounds = 1800 pounds! *Point out that 1800 pounds is nearly one ton; 1 ton = 2,240 pounds.* Then have students calculate the amount of PSI on a post of papers measuring 11" x 13" (1800÷143).

Finally, have students calculate the PSI when using a two–ton (or larger) hydraulic jack and compare the difference between man and machine!

Related Problem–Solving Activity

Turn this lesson into a problem–solving activity by having students come up with their own original techniques and devices for pressing paper as effectively and efficiently as possible.

Related Research Activity

Students can conduct research on Stanley Shetka, an artist living in Minnesota, who has invented an amazing paper press which can transform waste paper into "wood." (See the article "Paper Futures," in FIBERARTS, Volume 21, Number 3, November/December 1994.)

SCIENCE and MATHEMATICS: Studying Aerodynamics with Paper Airplanes and Kites

Books about paper airplanes are numerous. *Fabulous Paper Airplanes* by E. Richard Churchill does a good job of explaining the "science" of how they fly.

Beyond folding paper and making it fly, projects with paper airplanes can be related to the art curriculum in a variety of ways. Decorate the paper before making it into an airplane. Compare flying handmade paper airplanes with machine–made paper airplanes.

A related project would involve constructing and flying kites. Apply aerodynamic principles and address artistic concerns. The skill of using measuring tools is an important mathematical component of this activity. Kites have their own interesting history and group of books to read. *The Penguin Book of Kites* by David Pelham thoroughly covers the history, flying, and construction of kites. Kite–making fits perfectly into studies of Japan and China.

Mary Ballantyne, art teacher, shows Pete Waller the best place to tie his kite string for optimum aerodynamics.

MATHEMATICS: Mathematical Progression — Seeing Is Believing

Several books, including *The Amazing Paper Book* by Paulette Bourgeois and *Investigating Science with Paper* by Laurence B. White, Jr., suggest using paper as a dramatic way of teaching the concept of mathematical progression.

Mathematical progression can be illustrated by cutting paper.

1) Ask students for the number of times a piece of paper can be cut in half, restacking it each time, before the next cut is made.
2) Then have students test their hypothesis by actually cutting the paper.
3) Ten times may seem to be a reasonable number, but, as shown below, by the time the tenth cut is made, students will be attempting to cut 512 sheets of paper!

You can offer a variation of this activity by asking students how many times they could FOLD a piece of paper in half.

Some students might think the experiment will work if they use a giant sheet of paper. Let them try — and find out that it's impossible to fold 512 pages in half, no matter how big the paper is!

Cuts	*Sheets of Paper*
0	1
1	2
2	4
3	8
4	16
5	32
6	64
7	128
8	256
9	512
10	1024

Table of mathematical progression

SOCIAL STUDIES: Research and Map Skills

On a world map, mark the date when papermaking began in various countries to show how the knowledge of papermaking spread from China to Europe. *(See next page.)*

A reproducible map is located in the Appendix.

Dates (which were not always in agreement) for the chronologies on the following page were obtained from these books:

Papermaking: The History and Technique of an Ancient Craft by Dard Hunter
Papermaking by Jules Heller
Papermaking: The Art and Craft of Handmade Paper by Ralf Weidenmüller

On a map of the United States, mark the dates when papermaking began in the various states. Perhaps your state's historical society would have information on early papermaking in your state to research. See Appendix for a reproducible map.

The Journey of Papermaking

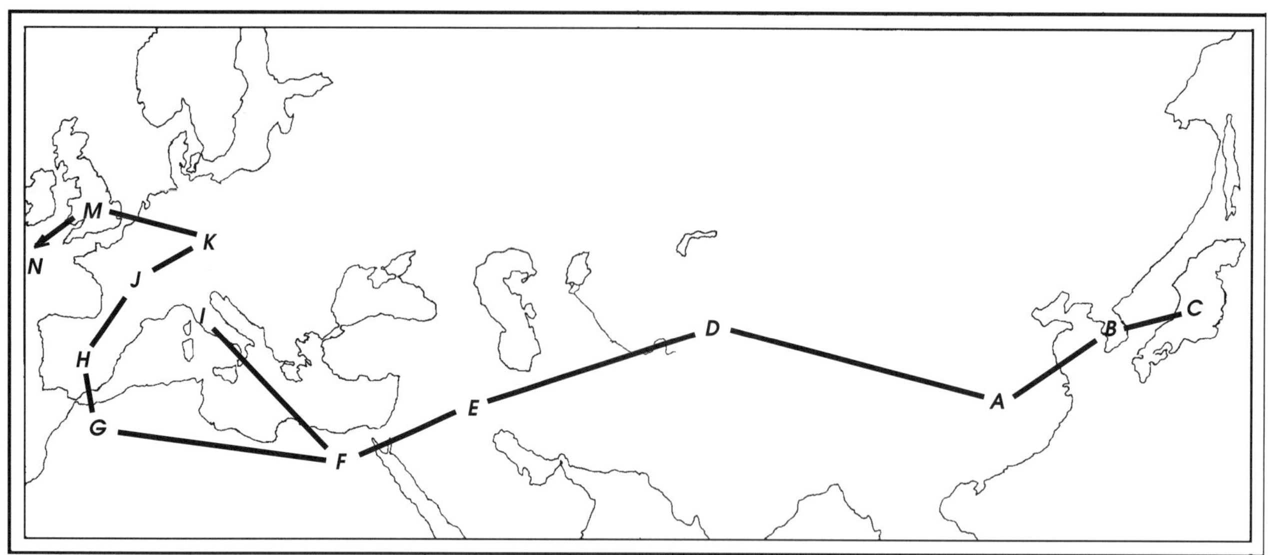

A 105 – China
B 600 – Korea
C 610-625 – Japan
D 751 – Samarkand
E 794 – Baghdad
F 900 – Egypt
G 1100 – Morocco
H 1150 – Spain
I 1268 – Italy
J 1348 – France
K 1390 – Germany
1411 – Switzerland
1428 – Holland
1491 – Poland
M 1494 – England
1498 – Austria
1499 – Bohemia
1546 – Hungary
1575-1578 – Mexico
1576 – Russia
1591 – Scotland
1635 – Denmark
1690 – Norway
N 1690 – United States

1690 – Pennsylvania
1726-1728 – New Jersey
1728 – Massachusetts
1734 – Maine
1744 – Virginia
1765 – Rhode Island
1767 – Connecticut
1769-1773 – New York
1776 – Maryland
1777 – North Carolina
1787 – Delaware
1790-1795 – Vermont
1792 – New Hampshire
1793 – Kentucky
1807 – Ohio
1810 – Georgia, S Carolina

1811? – Tennessee
1826 – Indiana
1834 – Missouri, Michigan
1840 – Illinois
1848 – Wisconsin
1849 – Alabama
1854 – Utah
1856-1857 – California
1859 – Minnesota
1866 – Oregon, Iowa
1874 – Kansas
1881 – Nebraska
1885 – Washington
1891 – Colorado
1898 – Louisiana
1900 – Florida

Social Studies:

A SHORT, CONCISE, YET VERY ENTERTAINING HISTORY OF HAND PAPERMAKING

(to be read aloud in the classroom!)

pre–paper:
American Indians used animal skins as a drawing and writing surface

PRE–PAPER

Many, many years ago, before figuring out how to make paper, people experimented with a variety of materials for writing and drawing. Some people painted on stone with a paint made from dirt and animal fat. Others carved words into stone using a chisel and mallet. Imagine writing a 200–word essay with a chisel and a mallet. Just try erasing a mistake! Another writing surface some people used was clay. Writing on clay tablets was much easier than chiseling in stone if it was done while they were wet, but clay tablets were a bit heavy to carry around. Wouldn't it be fun to lug a clay tablet to and from school in your backpack!

Wooden tablets covered with wax were also used for writing. By coating the board with a new layer of wax, it could be used many times. Two other early writing surfaces, parchment and vellum, were made from animal skins. To prepare the skin, the hair and fat was removed, the skin was stretched and scraped, and finally, the skin was dusted with powdered chalk and rubbed with pumice to make it smooth enough to write on.

Papyrus was the first writing surface made from a plant and its qualities were similar to those of paper. The word paper comes from the word papyrus, although papyrus is not true paper. To make papyrus, the plant is cut into thin strips and soaked. One layer of strips are laid side by side. Then another layer is laid in the opposite direction across the first. The layers are pressed together and dried.

Ts'ai Lun invents paper in China

TS'AI LUN

Although there is no absolute proof, credit for the invention of paper is given to Ts'ai Lun in China in the year 105 A.D. The story of Ts'ai's life varies somewhat from one history book to another. Back in those days, keeping accurate historical records was difficult because materials like paper, and tools like printing presses, typewriters or computers didn't exist. With all the tools and materials available today, the job of being a historian is much easier.

Here is one of the more entertaining versions of Ts'ai Lun's story. Ts'ai Lun was a peasant who served in the court of the emperor. Queen Dun-Shi, a great scholar, supervised Ts'ai Lun. She spent endless hours reading the classics, which were written on scrolls of silk. She cared little for gold, gems or jewels and would only accept silk paper as a gift. Because silk paper was so costly, she ordered Ts'ai Lun to create a cheaper and more plentiful writing material.

Ts'ai Lun worked constantly for many years to create a new writing material for the Queen, stopping only to eat and sleep. He finally developed a formula that combined the bark from a mulberry tree, scraps of linen, hemp, and fishing nets. Ts'ai Lun soaked this mixture in a large vat of water. Next, he beat it with a heavy club until the fibers came apart, and put the fibers in a vat of water. Then, he made a mould of loosely woven cloth stretched over a wooden frame. Finally, he dipped this mould into the vat of fibers and scooped up the pulp. Ts'ai Lun gently tilted the mould back and forth, and from side to side, evenly spreading the pulp. When the water had drained through the cloth, he set the mould in the sun to dry. When the pulp was dry, the matted fibers were pulled away from the cloth and became a piece of paper!

With his creation of paper, Ts'ai Lun was elevated to a higher position in the court. Later in his career, the Empress To ordered him to spread evil rumors about the royal family. He did as he was told. Unfortunately, the Empress fell out of power. Her successor, unhappy with Ts'ai Lun's gossiping, ordered him to appear before a judge. Ts'ai was so ashamed of what he had done that he drank poison and died.

PAPERMAKING SPREADS TO THE WESTERN WORLD

For over 700 years, the knowledge of papermaking was kept top secret. But in 751 A.D., an Arab army defeated the Chinese at Samarkand and took a number of skilled papermakers as prisoners. The captors put their prisoners to work making paper. The skill spread first to Damascus, then to Egypt and finally, to Europe. The first European mill was established either in Spain or in Italy around 1151. When it was introduced in Europe, paper was looked upon with suspicion, not only because it was higher priced and more fragile than parchment, but because paper was introduced by Jews, whom the Europeans did not trust because of religious differences, and by the Arabs, with whom they were always at war. Kings, nobles, and church officials in many places forbade the use of paper for important documents, saying that only parchment was good enough for "official" records.

MECHANICAL BEATERS

European papermakers made improvements in the process of papermaking. Instead of tearing up rags with muscle

Stamping mill

power, Europeans built stamping mills, where stamping machines were run by water–powered wheels. The Dutch started making paper in the seventeenth century, but they couldn't use stampers because the land was so flat, no streams had a strong enough current to turn a waterwheel. Around 1680, however, some clever Dutchman invented a machine to take the place of the stamper. This machine ran on wind power and came to be known as the Hollander beater.

FIRST PAPER MILLS IN UNITED STATES

The first paper mill in North America was established by William Rittenhouse in 1690, near Philadelphia, Pennsylvania. The second mill was established in 1710 by William De Weese, and a third one, built by Thomas Willcox, appeared

Colonists were urged to save their rags for making paper

in 1729. The British did not approve of paper mills in the Colonies. Before mills were started in North America, England was the only source for paper. However, nothing was done to stop the mills, because the English government knew the shortage of rags would limit the amount of paper that could be produced in the Colonies.

Although the Chinese method of papermaking was known throughout the civilized world, one important piece of information was either ignored or forgotten. The Chinese used mulberry bark and other plants to make their paper, but this part of their process (which would have solved the rag shortage problem) was lost to the Western world for almost two thousand years.

RAG SHORTAGE

Because Western countries made their paper from rags, when the demand for paper increased, the demand for rags increased and a shortage of rags was created. Different countries dealt with this rag shortage problem in a variety of ways. Germany and England ruled that dead bodies must be wrapped in wool, instead of the usual linen and cotton. In America, advertising campaigns were started to help ease the shortage. One newspaper ad stated: "Kind friend, when thy old shirt is rent, Let it to the paper mill be sent." Another ad begged housewives to make a rag bag for collecting scraps and hang it under the family Bible. Gifts were offered in exchange for rags. In Massachusetts, the price of rags rose from three pence a pound in 1777 to eight pence in 1778, to twelve pence two shillings by 1779 and it rose to ten shillings a pound by 1781. Tin peddlers now accepted rags in place of

Unwrapping mummies for the linen to use in making paper

money. As the campaign to save rags progressed, England became concerned and passed laws to limit the amount of paper the colonists could make.

REVOLUTIONARY WAR

During the Revolutionary War, the British completely stopped exporting paper to the Colonies. The paper shortage caused terrible confusion in George Washington's armies. Without paper, commanding officers could not issue written orders. Even the soldiers in the ranks suffered, since they needed paper to wrap powder and bullets for loading muskets. The situation became so desperate that every soldier who was a papermaker was discharged from the army to make paper.

MUMMY PAPER

One of the most unusual solutions to the rag shortage in the 1850's and 1860's was used by several American papermakers, including I. Augustus Stanwood and William Tower of Maine. Stanwood and Tower learned that there was a huge supply of ancient mummies in Egypt, each wrapped in many yards of fine linen. Egyptian railroads were using the mummies to stoke their locomotives. Papermakers began importing mummies in large quantities and stripping off the linen bandages to make pulp. One mummy could yield as much as thirty pounds of linen! The case of one Egyptian princess yielded forty–two yards of linen bandage. Mummy cases also included those of sacred cats, bulls, and crocodiles. Importing mummies was economical because rags in the United States cost four to six cents a pound in the 1860's,

René de Reaumur studied wasps making paper-like nests from wood fibers and suggested wood as a source for making paper

while linen from mummies sold for three cents a pound. Unfortunately, mummy wrappings caused an epidemic of cholera among the paper workers in a Maine mill, because the linen had never been disinfected.

Papermakers experimented with all kinds of different materials to replace rags, including tree moss, sugar cane, grapevine bark, potato skins, cabbage stalks, Indian corn, okra stems, and straw. Material for papermaking needed to be plentiful and inexpensive.

RENE DE REAUMUR

Early in the eighteenth century, well–known French naturalist and physicist René de Reaumur was studying wasps and noticed that their nests were made of a sort of paper. The wasps find old fences and shingles with wood fibers they can chew into a powder. By mixing this powder with an adhesive produced in their own body, these insects create a fine pulp which eventually transforms itself into many layers of paper while a nest is created.

On November 15, 1719, René de Reaumur reported to the French Royal Academy that:

"The American wasps form very fine paper, like ours; they extract the fibres of common wood of the countries where they live. They teach us that paper can be made from the fibres of plants without the use of rags and linen, and seem to invite us to try whether we cannot make fine and good paper from the use of certain woods. If we had woods similar to those used by the American wasps for their paper, we could make the whitest paper, for this material is very white.

By a further beating and breaking of the fibres that the wasps make and using the thin paste that comes from them, a very fine paper may be composed. This study should not be neglected, for it is, I dare say, important. The rags from which we make our paper are not an economical material and every papermaker knows that this substance is becoming rare. While the consumption of paper increases every day, the production of linen remains about the same. In addition to this, the foreign mills draw upon us for material. The wasp seems to teach us a means of overcoming these difficulties."

The speech was applauded and published, but nothing came of it, which should not be surprising, since new and revolutionary ideas are often slow to take root. Most people find change is hard and new ideas are very difficult to accept.

CHARLES FENERTY

In 1839, more than a hundred years after René de Reaumur announced his discovery, the Canadian youth Charles Fenerty began to build a machine for turning wood into pulp. After five years of trying, he succeeded in making one sheet of paper from the pulp. Fenerty's machine worked, but not very efficiently.

FRIEDRICH GOTTLOB KELLER

In 1844, Friedrich Gottlob Keller received a patent for a wood-grinding machine that worked. Keller got his idea while watching children making beads from cherry pits. In order to flatten and polish the pits, the youngsters secured them on a notched block of wood and rubbed them against a grindstone. Where the block rubbed against the stone, friction caused wood fibers to fall away. When he picked up the fibers, Keller found they were moist and that they matted together in layers, just as the rag fibers did in papermaking. From this time forward, wood was used more and more often as a source for paper pulp, and on January 15, 1863, the entire edition of The Boston Weekly Journal was printed on "paper made of wood, a new process."

THE PAPER ERA

During and following the Civil War, experiments involving the manufacture of all types of articles made from paper and research into wood–fiber development took place. In 1853, the first paper collars and cuffs were seen in New York City. Ten years later, paper was being used to make waistcoats, bonnets, aprons, hats, tapestry, curtains, carpets, roofing, building materials, boxes, buckets, cuspidors, and barrels. In 1870, a London music hall featured a song called "The Age of Paper," sung by Mr. Howard Paul, "attired in a suit of paper."

Cover of sheet music with Howard Paul, appearing in paper clothes

The workman on the left, called a vatman, formed the sheet of paper on the mould, and passed the mould to the coucher (on the right), who turned the mould over onto the felt. The third worker in the papermaking process was the layman, whose job it was to remove the paper from the felts after it had been pressed, and then return the felts to the vatman.

CONDITIONS FOR EARLY PAPERMAKERS

Along with the shortage of rags, the length of time and the amount of hard work required to make a sheet of paper was a problem. Early papermakers labored twelve hours a day in dark, wet rooms, their faces buried in the steam from vats, their arms continually plunged into warm, pulpy water and their backs bowed, as they stooped over piles of paper. It's small wonder that papermakers had the reputation of being hard-drinking and quarrelsome.

The workmen often lived in the mill itself or in cottages nearby, and took meals at the master's table. In Holland, custom decreed that the men must stop eating whenever the master showed he had finished by laying down his spoon. Some stingy mill owners were even said to have their workmen's food served so hot that they could eat very little of it before the master finished his cooler bowl and laid down his spoon. As a result, the men gulped their food hastily. For many years after this period, a Dutch mother, on seeing her child wolf down his dinner, would ask him whether he thought he was a papermaker.

NICHOLAS–LOUIS ROBERT

Around 1798, Nicholas–Louis Robert, a worker in the Didot paper mill in France, decided to build a machine that would make paper. Robert's idea did not come from a desire to make paper faster and cheaper. According to his own words, his reason was disgust and impatience with the constant arguments he had with quarrelsome, short–tempered vatmen, couchers, and laymen in the mill. Robert, encouraged by his employer Leger Didot, spent all of his time away

A model of the first papermaking machine

from work trying to invent such a machine. His invention, though simple and crude, was the prototype for today's modern papermaking machine.

Robert applied for and received a patent for his invention. Because of the French Revolution, little progress was made with Robert's papermaking machine. Robert was having financial problems and so he sold his patent to Didot for 25,000 francs. Didot was slow to pay Robert, and in 1801, Robert took back his patent.

FOURDRINIER

Didot moved to England in 1801, where he enlisted the help of two London stationers, Henry and Sealy Fourdrinier. The Fourdrinier brothers hired an engineer, Dryan Donkin, to build a new and improved version of Robert's machine and within four years, they were marketing this new machine. The first paper machine in the United States was built by Donkin and shipped to Henry Barclay's mill in 1827. Of the four men, only Donkin obtained any wealth. Because of a flaw in their patent, the Fourdrinier brothers never received a penny from the users of the machine. Although both Didot and the Fourdrinier brothers went bankrupt, today's papermaking machine is still called a Fourdrinier.

Life did not immediately become easier for owners of the new Fourdrinier machines. Owners soon encountered violent opposition from workers. Frightened that their jobs would disappear, the men rioted and attacked the mills. The mill windows had to be boarded up, and one owner placed bottles of vitriol, a powerful acid, on the roof of his mill, ready to pour on the heads of rioting workers. However, the machines soon created such increased demand for paper that more, rather than fewer, workers were needed. As you can see, history repeats itself. Over and over again, people tend to resist change.

DARD HUNTER

About the time of the Civil War, making paper by hand had pretty much become extinct. However, a small number of people remained interested in papermaking. Dard Hunter, perhaps the most important figure in reviving the art of hand papermaking in this century, set up a hand papermaking mill in Lime Rock, Connecticut in 1928. Hunter also travelled throughout the world, writing books about how paper was made and collecting all kinds of tools and materials related to papermaking. You can see his collection at the American Museum of Papermaking, if you are ever in Atlanta, Georgia. Along with others such as Douglass Morse Howell, who was the first papermaker to experiment with the creative possibilities of paper in and of itself, Dard Hunter planted the seeds that have blossomed over the last 20 years into hand papermaking becoming a major new medium in the world of art.

Information for this history was obtained from the following books: *Papermaking in the Classroom* by Dard Hunter; *Paper* by Jerome S. Meyers; *The Magic of Paper* by Walter Buehr; *The Papermakers* by Leonard Everett Fisher; *Paper* by Elizabeth Simpson Smith; *Papermaking* by Jules Heller; *Papermaking: The History and Technique of an Ancient Craft* by Dard Hunter.

SOCIAL STUDIES: How Proto–Paper is Made in Various Cultures*

Many cultures have a distinctive method of making paper or proto–paper, which allows papermaking to fit well into multicultural studies.

During her sixth grade year, my daughter researched and gave a presentation to her class on the Mayan culture. As part of her report, she demonstrated how to make amate, the ancient writing material used by the Maya.

Around the same time, I was asked to make a presentation to an elementary school class during their study of Egypt. Egyptians are widely thought to have made the first paper, but papyrus is technically different than what we know as paper.

By referring to Lillian Bell's book *Papyrus, Tapa, Amate, and Rice Paper,* I was able to figure out how to make both amate and papyrus. Her instructions are very clear and are accompanied with detailed illustrations. Bell also lists sources for plant materials for making these proto–papers.

Papermaking techniques from countries and areas of the world described in Bell's book include Egypt, Uganda, Polynesia, the Brazilian Amazon, pre–Columbian and present–day Mexico, Indonesia, Southern China and Taiwan.

Sophie Dawson provides "how to" information on papyrus and amate in her book, *The Art and Craft of Papermaking*. Information on this topic can also be found in Sheryl Cunning's book *Oriental and Western Papermaking.*

*The term proto–papers refers to writing and painting surfaces which are similar to "true" paper.

amate paper

This image is from a bas–relief carved by the ancient Mayans of Chiapas, Mexico. It depicts an important ceremony, where Jaguar Shield (on the right), the king of Yaxchitlan in 630 A.D., offers the serpent scepter (the symbol of wisely used power), to his maiden, who, in turn, offers her receptive vase of water in exchange. The image was serigraphed on paper handmade by Mayan craftsmen in Yucatan. The paper was made from renewable resources, such as bowstring hemp and banana fiber, using a combination of Oriental and Mayan techniques. Both of these fibers are cultivated and used ecologically instead of tree bark, which, if used excessively, can cause irreparable damage to the natural environment.

Courtesy of Project Huun, Mexico
Mark Callaghan, Project Director

SOCIAL STUDIES and LANGUAGE ARTS: Historical Research, Writing and Speaking

Students can research, write a report and present their findings to the class about the following people and their relationship to paper. Information on these important people can be found in many of the books listed in the Bibliography.

Besides providing students a chance to practice their research skills, this assignment gives students some insight into the life of an inventor and creates an appreciation for some of the paper products we take so much for granted, such as Kleenex™ and paper bags. Following are some people for students to research:

René Antoine Ferchault de Reaumur
observed wasps making their hives and proposed that paper could be made from certain woods, but was ignored

Johann Gutenberg
invented the printing press, which increased the need for paper

Ts'ai Lun
a Chinese peasant credited with discovering papermaking

Nicholas–Louis Robert
a Frenchman who invented the first papermaking machine

Fourdrinier Brothers
built a new and improved paper machine patterned after Robert's; today's papermaking machine is still called the fourdrinier

John Dickinson
created and perfected the first rotary papermaking machine in 1809

Friedrich Gottlob Keller
in 1844, patented a wood-grinding machine; developed his idea while watching small children make beads from cherry pits

William Rittenhouse
set up first papermill in the United States

Benjamin Franklin
encouraged papermills to thrive; used much paper in his printing and publishing business

Matthias Koops
published a book in 1880, part of which was printed on paper made of wood pulp; went bankrupt trying to win acceptance for this new process

Charles Fenerty
a Canadian youth who, in 1839, began building a machine that would turn wood into pulp; after five years of work, he succeeded in making one sheet of paper

Sir Henry Cole
"invented" the Christmas card

Francis Wolle
invented a bagmaking machine

Charles Stillwell
invented a machine to produce square–bottomed bags

Colonel Edward L. Mills

perfected a paper "sandwich," in which tiny red and blue silk threads were imbedded

Dard Hunter (1883–1966)

practiced, studied, and wrote about the method and history of papermaking; was instrumental in reviving the practice of hand papermaking in the 20th century

RELATED ASSIGNMENT I:

Just about everyone I know is interested in money. Students can do research on how paper money is made. They can find good information on this topic by writing to the United States Department of the Treasury.

RELATED ASSIGNMENT II:

Students can research machine papermaking both in the library and by writing letters to paper companies for information. To find addresses of paper companies, refer to the *Lockwood–Post's Directory*, which is listed in the section *Suppliers and Other Useful Resources.*

SOCIAL STUDIES and LANGUAGE ARTS: Reading and History

Most books written about hand papermaking include a short history. Assign students to read about the history of papermaking from the following sources:

ELEMENTARY

The Amazing Paper Book by Paulette Bourgeois, pages 8–9, 12–15, 18–21, 24–25, 28, 32–33.
Papermaking in the Classroom by Dard Hunter, pages 7–47.
Paper by Kids by Arnold E. Grummer, pages 24–31.
Paper by Jerome S. Meyers, pages 18–38.
The Magic of Paper by Walter Buehr, pages 11–59.
How Paper is Made by Lesley Perrins, pages 16–21.
The New World of Paper by Irmengarde Eberle, pages 21–29.
The Papermakers by Leonard Everett Fisher, pages 7–41.
Paper by Elizabeth Simpson Smith, pages 16–38.

SECONDARY

The Wonderful World of Paper by Angelo Cohn, pages 15–38.
Papermaking in the Classroom by Dard Hunter, pages 7–47.
The Art and Craft of Handmade Paper by Vance Studley, pages 10–26.
The Art of Papermaking by Bernard Toale, pages 2–6.
Japanese Papermaking by Timothy Barrett, pages 7–19.
Papermaking by Jules Heller, pages 23–31, 185–89.
The Art and Craft of Papermaking by Sophie Dawson, pages 8–15.
Paper Pleasures by Faith Shannon, pages 8–16.
Papermaking: The History and Technique of an Ancient Craft by Dard Hunter.
Decorative Papers by Diane Maurer–Mathison, pages 12–15.
Recycled Papers: The Essential Guide by Claudia G. Thompson, pages 21–35.

RELATED ASSIGNMENT: Students can make a time line, marking the important developments in the history of papermaking.

SOCIAL STUDIES and LANGUAGE ARTS: A Visual Story

Artistic works often tell a story. Such work is called narrative art. Students can learn about content in art through seeing examples of other's work and by creating their own. Following are a few of many possible examples and their sources:

Squares from the NAMES Project quilt
— from Ruskin, Cindy. *The Quilt, Stories from the NAMES Project.* New York: Pocket Books, 1988.

The Chess Game by George Tooker, 1956
Cat Seizing Bird by Pablo Picasso, 1939
Cat and Bird by Paul Klee, 1928
Paris Through the Window by Marc Chagall, 1913
— from Roalf, Peggy. *Looking at Paintings/Cats.* New York: Hyperion Books for Children, 1992.

Little Girl in a Blue Armchair by Mary Cassatt, 1879
The Piano Lesson by Henri Matisse, 1916
Children's Games by Pieter Bruegel, 1560
Dream of a Sunday Afternoon in the Alameda by Diego Rivera, 1947–48
— from Richmond, Robin. *The Story in a Picture: Children in Art.* Nashville, Tennessee: Ideals Children's Books, 1992.

The Loveletter by Jan Vermeer, 1669–70
The Agony in the Garden by Andrea Mantegna, ca. 1460
The Scream by Edvard Munch, 1893
Harriet Tubman Series by Jacob Lawrence, 1939–40
— from Pekarik, Andrew. *Painting Behind the Scenes.* New York: Hyperion Books for Children, 1992.

Black Girl's Window by Betye Saar, 1969
The Liberation of Aunt Jemima by Betye Saar, 1972
Grandmother Moorhead's Aromatic Kitchen by Leonora Carrington, 1975
— from Sills, Leslie. *Visions: Stories About Women Artists.* Morton Grove, Illinois: Albert Whitman & Company, 1993.

Students can use stories they have already written or they can write a story and translate it into a visual piece, using both paper and pulp, with the option of incorporating either words and/or script into their pieces.

You could also choose mixed media, with paper as one of the mediums, for this project.

"Calvin"
by
the author

with text by her daughter,
Laurel Kirstein Smith
at age 8

complete text found on following pages

CALVIN

Text from the cover art work, written by Laurel Kirstein Smith at age eight.

One day I was up in my room reading *Matilda* for the tenth time. (I've read it thirteen times now.) I went downstairs to call a friend and my dad was on the phone. He was talking to someone about a cocker spaniel. He said, "Oh well I'll call someone else" and he hung up.

"What was that all about?" I said.

"I was on the phone with someone in the paper who was selling a cocker spaniel but someone took him yesterday," he said.

He made a couple more calls and then he called someone who had eight cocker spaniel black labrador retriever puppies. My brother was at his friend Tyler's house so we called him up and told him and said that Tyler could come with us if he wanted to. He didn't so we picked up Nathan and went to see the puppies.

When we got there my mom and dad were looking for the house they almost moved into but when they saw it they realized that it was where the puppies were too. So after a while we decided on one of them. It wasn't quite the one my dad wanted because the one he wanted was the runt. He wanted the runt because it wouldn't get as big and because it had the shortest hair so it would be easier to groom but it wasn't interested in people as much as the other ones were so we decided to get Calvin because for once Nathan and I actually agreed on one and because he was the second smallest one. The people who owned him named him Trouble. Well anyway in the car Nathan got to hold him. He was on his lap on the way home. He was sort of shy when we first got him but not that shy really. He's gotten much much bolder. In fact for example a couple of days ago while my brother and dad were doing the paper route Calvin would never go up the steps with them so they usually just tie the leash to the wagon handle until they get back down the steps. But one day he just ran down Bever (Avenue) with the wagon! Then my dad had to chase him. Just then my brother came back from delivering to a house around the corner and saw my dad running down Bever but he didn't see Calvin running with the wagon so he yelled "DAD WHAT ARE YOU DOING?" But he didn't answer until he got Calvin.

My grandma and grandpa were having a big dance for their 40 somethingth anniversary and all of their friends and neighbors and relatives were coming so we dropped Calvin off at someone's house. Her name was Kate and she had a full grown Black Lab and they got along just fine. They were playing and having fun but the other dog slept inside and Calvin usually slept outside so Kate let Calvin outside in the backyard and Calvin got lonely. He wanted to go home because he didn't know we were gone. He thought we had just abandoned him so he found a way out of the fence and went two or three blocks and he got ran over by a car.

The person who ran him over didn't know they ran over anything. At 5:00 in the morning someone was driving to work and they saw Calvin so they called the police and the Animal Shelter. He was only unconscious but there was really nothing they could do about it. But of course we were still at my grandma and grandpa's house and Kate was still sleeping so she didn't even know Calvin was gone yet and by the time she found out he was gone he was a "dead doggie." So she left a message on the answering machine and when we got back we didn't go pick up Calvin because it was 11:00 at night so Kate would be sleeping so we were going to pick up Calvin in the morning. Nathan and I went straight to bed because of course it was 11:00 and we would normally go to bed at 9:30 and after we were both in bed my mom and dad went down to check the messages on the answering machine and heard the message about Calvin. So in the morning my mom told my brother and he couldn't stop crying but I was still sound asleep. When I woke up my brother was still bawling his head off and my mom had woke me up and I asked "Have we picked Calvin up yet?"

My mom said "He got out somehow." Then I started crying but she didn't say he got hit yet but when she did I started crying even more and more. I didn't go to school that morning and my mom didn't blame me. She looked into the ads to see if there were any good dogs for sale. At first my brother didn't want another dog but we talked him into it and then he wanted one.

Finally we went to school at about 11:30 and had just ate lunch at home and when we got there the class looked like a tornado had just hit. My brother said "Whoa."

I said "They are working on their Pilgrim and Indian costumes." But there was nobody in the room so we decided that we would drop off my brother at his classroom and on the way we saw my class lining up for lunch so I joined my class but as I said earlier I had already eaten lunch at home so I sat through lunch without eating anything at all. I kept saying "This is so boring." We were sitting across from another class and they told on me for not having a lunch but I didn't get into trouble because I explained to them that I already ate lunch.

When I got home my mom was still crying but someone she had called in Anamosa that picked up stray dogs because there wasn't an animal shelter in Anamosa and she said she had a very nice dog and it was free and its name was Katie. She liked to lick people's faces a lot so we decided to get her. She's a lot of fun. We like to play football with her. A couple of days ago we got her spayed. She's still tired a lot and they had to shave her belly in order to have her surgery. The end.

*SOCIAL STUDIES, LANGUAGE ARTS, MATHEMATICS, and SCIENCE: **Brainstorming***

Learning to brainstorm improves awareness, fosters creativity, and has important applications to all subject areas.

Young students can brainstorm in a single group, with the teacher listing their answers on the board. Older students can break up into small groups and create separate lists to present to the rest of the class.

Brainstorm Idea I: How many uses for paper can you think of?

Brainstorm Idea II: How many different kinds of paper can you think of?

Brainstorm Idea III: What might be some future uses for paper?

Variation on Brainstorming Theme:

Ask students to bring to school examples of the many ways paper is used, such as tissue, wrapping paper, cereal boxes, and so forth. Make a display of the items.

Writing Activity:

Students can write about the many uses of paper. At left are some examples of this assignment from papers written by students in Ms. Timm's fifth grade class at Pierce Elementary School in Cedar Rapids, Iowa in March 1994.

Brainstorming idea:
the many uses of paper

• "It is used for punch cards and paper airplanes. People use it for computer print outs, disk labels, and paper bags. It is used in big books and in little books. Paper is used for posters, paper cups, barf bags, work sheets, playing cards, diaries, coffee filters, tea bags, lunch bags, paper making, trash, litter, traffic tickets, parking tickets, legal documents, and sports cards."
Weston Lahr

• "Sometimes it's good to have paper like when you get a present and other times it's not like when you do something bad at school and you might get a note home for your parents."
Zach Paulson

• "One of my favorite kinds of paper is crepe paper. It is fun to use and fun to decorate with and it comes in so many neat colors."
Kelly Trask

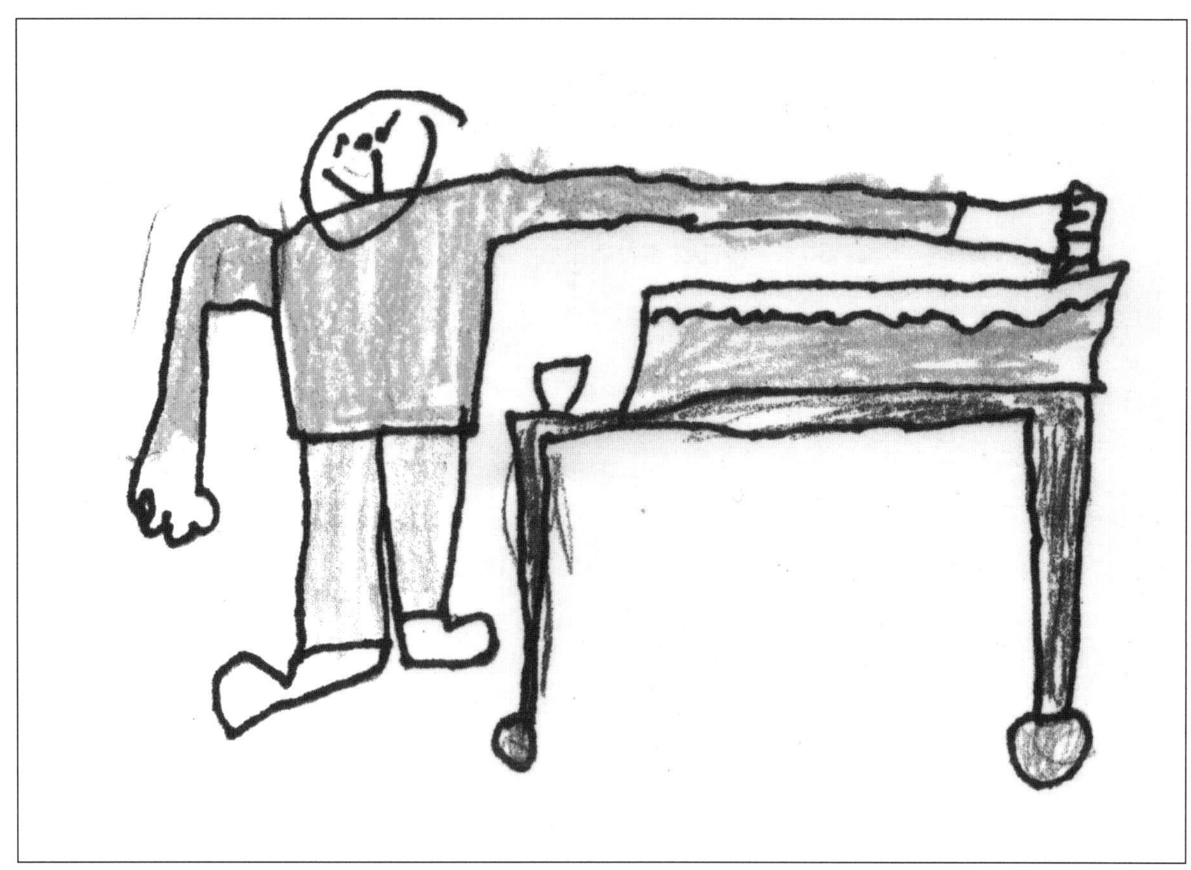

***thank-you note drawing to the author
by
William Moore
age 6***

Mar. 31, 1994

Dear Mrs. Smith,

Thank you for shoing me how to mac papre. I had a fun fun time. The papre felt like goy, but it was still fun.

William Moore

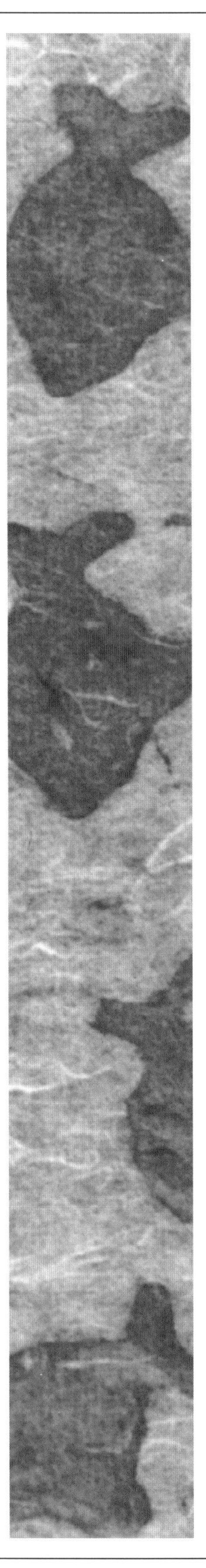

Annotated Bibliography

When I first started gathering information and ideas to supplement my papermaking residencies in the schools, I was amazed at the number of books about papermaking that I found in the childrens' section of the Cedar Rapids Public Library. Through Interlibrary Loan, I found and reviewed as many as I could get my hands on. I know that many more books are out there than I have had a chance to read, but I hope this list helps you provide books your students can read independently, and that you can use as resources.

BOOKS

Papermaking for Young Readers

Asimov, Isaac and Elizabeth Kaplan. *How is Paper Made*. Milwaukee: Gareth Stevens Publishing. 1993. 23 pages. Tells how paper is made by machine and covers recycling. Short enough to read aloud to elementary school children. Pictures on every page.

Bourgeois, Paulette. *The Amazing Paper Book*. Reading, Massachusetts: Addison–Wesley Publishing Company, Inc. 1990. 79 pages. Written for 7– to 11–year–olds. Covers a wide range of information and activities relating to paper, including why paper is important, the history of papermaking, writing and printing on paper, how to cook a dinner in parchment paper, paper inventions of toilet paper, paper bags, facial tissues, cartons and carbon paper, block printing, pop–up cards, wasps, math and science brain–teasers using paper, logging, forest farming, a modern paper mill, how a newspaper is made, recycling, scientific information about trees.

Buehr, Walter. *The Magic of Paper*. New York: William Morrow and Company. 1966. 95 pages. For children. History of papermaking with special emphasis on the development of tools and techniques. Discusses watermarks, modern machine papermaking, and conversion of paper into other products like corrugated cardboard. Speculates on the future of papermaking (some activities now occurring, since this book was written in 1966).

Coob, Vicki. *The Secret Life of School Supplies*. New York: J.B. Lippincott. 1981. 14 pages written about paper. Briefly covers the history of hand papermaking and machine papermaking, offers experiments for learning about paper qualities of absorption, density, tensile strength, grain, brightness, opacity, curl, and watermarks.

Cosner, Shaaron. *"Paper" through the Ages*. Minneapolis, Minnesota: Carolrhoda Books. 1984. 48 pages. For elementary students. Discusses various surfaces that have been used for writing, including stone, clay, papyrus, wax, parchment, and finally, paper.

Dineen, Jacqueline. *Wood and Paper*. Hillside, New Jersey: Enslow Publishers, Inc. 1988. 31 pages. Written for children. Tells how trees are taken from forests, how forests are cared for, what happens to wood at the sawmill, modern machine papermaking, and the many paper products and uses for paper.

Eberle, Irmengarde. *The New World of Paper*. New York: Dodd, Mead & Company. 1969. 95 pages. Topics include the uses of paper, its history, and how machine–made paper is made, starting with the logging operation.

Fisher, Leonard Everett. *The Papermakers*. New York: Franklin Watts, Inc. 1965. 46 pages, many pictures. Written for children. Discusses the history and technique of early American hand papermaking. Suitable for reading aloud to a class or for use as a resource. Very appropriate when studying the colonial period of American history.

Fletcher, Helen Jill, and Seli Groves. *How On Earth Do We Recycle Paper?* Brookfield, Connecticut: The Millbrook Press. 1992. 63 pages. Topics include a brief history of papermaking, how machine–made paper is made today, problems with filling our landfills with paper, and how to reduce, reuse and recycle the paper we use. Suggestions for what students can do to get politically involved and a section of projects using paper that might otherwise be thrown away.

Grummer, Arnold. *Paper by Kids*. Minneapolis: Dillon Press, Inc. 1990. Includes simple instructions for making paper and papermaking tools. A plan for an easy, inexpensive press is included. Also has a chapter on the science of papermaking and a chapter on the history of papermaking. Elementary level.

Grummer, Arnold. *Tin Can Papermaking, Recycle for Earth and Art*. Appleton, Wisconsin: Greg Markim Publishers. 1992. 80 pages. Emphasizes recycling. Simple methods are possibilities for "art on a cart" teachers. Good reference for students who want to make paper at home. Includes a chapter on how and why the fibers bond together. Photographs of magnified pieces of paper and a good chapter for integrating with the science curriculum.

How Things are Made. Washington D.C.: National Geographic Society. 1986. A brief 4–page explanation of how paper is made by machine is included in this book.

Macaulay, David. *The Way Things Work*. Boston: Houghton Mifflin Company. 1988. 384 pages. Topics related to papermaking include hydraulics, principles of flight (paper airplanes and kites), pressure gauges, printing process, machine papermaking, and bookbinding. Wonderful illustrations.

Meyer, Jerome S. *Paper*. New York: The World Publishing Company. 1960. 87 pages. Written for young people. Discusses the many ways that paper is used in our society, how its invention affected civilization, the history of papermaking, modern machine papermaking, simple explanations of the "science" of the process. Good photographs of a paper mill, conversion of paper into cardboard, and the making of money.

Perrins, Lesley. *How Paper is Made*. New York: Facts on File Publications. 1985. 32 pages. Written for young people, with excellent photographs and illustrations. Discusses the many uses and qualities of paper, modern machine papermaking, how different paper products are made, the history of papermaking, recycling, how to make handmade paper, and how to make an origami Samurai hat and a salt cellar. With glossary, facts and figures.

Smith, Elizabeth Simpson. *Paper*. New York: Walker and Company. 1984. 64 pages. Written for children. Discusses the many uses of paper, the history of papermaking, modern machine papermaking, watermarks.

Valentine, Malcolm, and Rosalind Dace. *How To Make Your Own Recycled Paper*. London: Market Ecology/Search Press. 1990. 32 pages. Covers the basics of using simple tools for recycling paper.

Paper–related, Young Readers

Aliki. *How a Book is Made*. New York: Thomas Y. Crowell. 1986. 32 pages. Takes the reader step by step through the process of writing and publishing a book. Contains lots of technical information presented in "cartoon" form, substituting cats for people, so it may seem less intimidating to children (and probably adults, as well).

Churchill, E. Richard. *Fabulous Paper Airplanes*. New York: Sterling Publishing Co., Inc. 1991. 128 pages. Directions for a variety of paper airplanes, with 246 illustrations. Explains the principles of aerodynamics in language understandable to children. Explains the basic principles of flight and gives folding instructions for 29 paper airplanes.

Churchill, E. Richard. *Paper Science Toys*. New York: Sterling Publishing Co., Inc. 1991. 128 pages. Introduces scientific principles (sound waves, center of gravity, light and sight, angles and circles, time and direction, force and motion, air pressure) through toys made of paper.

Feller, Ron and Marsha. *Paper Masks and Puppets*. Seattle: The Arts Factory. 1985. 101 pages. Written by art educators. Shows many examples and directions for creating both animal and human paper sculpture masks. Discusses paper sculpture techniques of scoring, curling, cutting, and folding, and offers suggestions for incorporating masks into the creation and performance of group stories, songs, and plays.

Honda, Isao. *The World of Origami*. San Francisco: Japan Publications Trading Company. 1965. 182 pages. An origami book with clear and easy–to–follow instructions.

Irvine, Joan. *How to Make Super Pop–ups*. New York: Morrow Junior Books. 1992. 96 pages. Written for children. Fun! Great ideas for cards, masks and books.

Jones Madeline. *The Mysterious Flexagons: An Introduction to a Fascinating New Concept in Paper Folding*. New York: Crown Publishers, Inc. 1966. 48 pages. Flexagons are described by the author as amusing little paper figures that mystify and fascinate the flexer and all who behold him. This book will be helpful for integrating math with a curriculum centered around paper.

Pellowski, Anne. *The Family Storytelling Handbook*. New York: Macmillan Publishing Co. 1987. 150 pages. Includes origami (paper folding) stories and paper–cutting or –tearing stories. Elementary level.

Purdy, Susan. *Books for You to Make*. New York: J.B. Lippincott Company. 1973. 96 pages. Contents include how to write a book, how to design a book, basic bookbinder skills, bookbinder's vocabulary, and how printed books are made.

Weiss, Harvey. *How to Make Your Own Books*. New York: Thomas Y. Crowell Company. 1974. 71 pages. Tells how to make a book and gives suggestions for a variety of different types of books to make.

White, Jr., Laurence B. *Investigating Science with Paper*. Reading, Massachusetts: Addison–Wesley Publishing Company. 1970. 123 pages. Lots of fun and interesting ideas for integrating papermaking with the science curriculum. Many experiments for discovering properties of paper, learning the scientific method and other scientific principles. Includes paper engineering activities, math magic tricks and problem–solving exercises.

General Papermaking

Barrett, Timothy. *Japanese Papermaking: Traditions, Tools and Techniques*. New York: Weatherhill. 1983. 317 pages. A thorough source book for people wanting to learn Japanese papermaking.

Bell, Lillian. *Plant Fibers for Papermaking*. McMinnville, Oregon: Liliaceae Press. 1981. A "recipe" book for preparing a variety of plant fibers for papermaking. Offers basic instructions, along with specific directions for preparing many different plant fibers.

Bell, Lillian. *Papyrus, Tapa, Amate & Rice Paper.* McMinnville, Oregon: Liliaceae Press. 1983. Explores the fibers and techniques used to make paper in Africa, the Pacific, Latin America, and Southeast Asia. Complements cultural studies of those areas.

Clark, James D'A. *Pulp Technology and Treatment for Paper.* San Francisco: Miller Freeman Publications. 878 pages. For teachers or advanced students wanting to learn more about the science of papermaking.

Cohn, Angelo. *The Wonderful World of Paper.* New York: Abelard–Schuman. 1967. 141 pages. Written for high school or adult readers. Includes history, how paper is made, the many uses of paper and various career opportunities in the paper industry.

Cunning, Sheryl. *Handmade Paper: Oriental and Western Papermaking.* Escondido, CA: Cunning Enterprises. 1989. 115 pages. Although I haven't been able to get my hands on a copy of this book to review, the descriptions I read in papermaker's supply catalogs sound like it would be a very valuable resource. The following information is from catalogs of Lee Scott McDonald and Twinrocker: "A step by step manual for beginning papermakers which includes beating, coloring, harvesting local plants, instructions for making Oriental and Nepalese paper, as well as papyrus, tapa and amate are given. Includes recipes for the commonly found materials and products being used today."

Dawson, Sophie. *The Art and Craft of Papermaking.* Philadelphia, Pennsylvania: Running Press. 1992. 144 pages. Color photographs of paper artwork by numerous artists; pictures of tools and techniques. Covers the basics, sculptural techniques, vacuum–forming, pulp spraying, pulp painting, watermarks, papyrus, collage, embossing, embedding, shibori and laminating. Glossary of papermaking terms. Ideas for projects such as bookbinding and monoprinting. Excellent resource for teachers.

Heller, Jules. *Papermaking.* New York: Watson–Guptill Publications. 1978. 216 pages. A good resource book. Covers history, definition of various types of paper, instructions on how to make paper, tools, how to produce the right kind of papers for needs such as printmaking or watercolor, recycling, and casting. An extensive gallery section features more than fifty artists. A section on papermaking for schools briefly covers several approaches for teaching children. Contains an extensive bibliography and list of suppliers. Large glossary of papermaking terms.

Hughes, Sukey. *Washi: The World of Japanese Paper.* New York: Kodansha International. 1978. 360 pages. This would be a very good reference book to have on hand when studying the Japanese culture. With over 100 photos showing the Japanese papermaking process, it is valuable to use in the classroom even as a picture book. Hughes covers history, how Japanese paper is made, people who make paper, different types of paper, and discusses how Washi is an expression of Japanese culture and craftsmanship, as well as an expression of Japan's ideals of beauty and an intense feeling for nature.

Hunter, Dard. Papermaking, *The History and Technique of an Ancient Craft.* New York: Dover Publications, Inc. 1978. 612 pages. Originally published in 1943, this comprehensive book covers the history and thoroughly examines the tools and materials of papermaking.

Hunter, Dard. *Papermaking in the Classroom.* New Castle, Delaware: Oak Knoll Books. 1991. 80 pages. Originally published in 1931, Hunter's was the first book of practical instruction for the amateur papermaker, written by the single most important figure in twentieth century American papermaking history. Written for children between the ages of 12 and 14, it covers the history of papermaking and tells students how to make their own paper from rags. Although the methods are not directly applicable to today's classroom, Hunter's book is of great historical interest.

Kropper, Jean G. *Papermaking from Recycling to Art.* Port Melbourne, Victoria, Australia: Lothian Books. 1992. 64 pages. An easy–to–read book covering the basics of papermaking. Also includes embossing, watermarks, casting, embedding, plant fibers, sizing; with color photos of art work in paper, and craft projects to make with papers.

Mitsukuni, Yoshida and Inumaru Tadashi, Editorial Supervisors. *The Traditional Crafts of Japan: Volume 7, Paper and Dolls.* Tokyo: Diamond, Inc. 1992. 189 pages. Gorgeous color photographs of Japanese handmade paper, with descriptions of the process and black–and–white photographs of making the paper. Volume 7 also covers fans, umbrellas, scrolls, dolls, drums, candles, banners and fishing flies.

Saddington, Marianne. *Making Your Own Paper.* Pownal, Vermont: Storey Communications, 1992. 93 pages. The author is a graphic designer, papermaker and calligrapher, with a special interest in the creative applications of lettering. A "project"–oriented book. Topics include basic papermaking, simple tools, preparing a writing surface, sizing, laminating, embossing, paper casting, making paper from plants. Projects include stationery, cards, collage, bags, boxes and bookbinding.

Stearns, Lynn. *Papermaking for Basketry*. Bayside, CA: Press de LaPlantz, Inc. 1988. 200 pages. Features papermaking and basketmaking techniques of seventeen basketmakers, with many photographs. Several artists discuss preparation of plant fibers. Papermaking suppliers, a bibliography, and a glossary of papermaking terms are included. A good resource for those interested in working three–dimensionally with paper.

Studley, Vance. *The Art & Craft of Handmade Paper*. New York: Van Nostrand Reinhold Company, Inc. 1977. 112 pages. Good source for learning how to make paper. Covered are a history of papermaking, tools and materials, processing of plant fibers, sheetforming, pressing and drying. Project section includes three–dimensional casting, embedding, layering, collage, making a portfolio, and making paper for printmaking and drawing. Many examples of paper artists' work. Bibliography and brief glossary.

Thompson, Claudia G. *Recycled Papers: The Essential Guide*. Cambridge, MA: The MIT Press. 1992. 162 pages. A resource book. Topics include the dimensions of the solid waste problem, the history of papermaking, the elements of recycled paper production and possibilities for the future.

Toale, Bernard. *The Art of Papermaking*. Worcester, Massachusetts: Davis Publications, Inc. 1983. 119 pages. Very good source for learning how to make paper. Topics include a history of papermaking, Eastern and Western papermaking, and papermaking from plants. Detailed chapter on sculptural techniques of plaster casting, spraying pulp, rubber molds, shaped molds, deckle box and vacuum–table casting. Excellent glossary of papermaking terms; suppliers' list and bibliography. Many examples of paper artists' work, including a section in color.

Todman, Tonia. *Tonia Todman's Paper–Making Book*. Rozelle, Australia: Sally Milner Publishing. 1992. 55 pages. Written by a craft editor.

Weidenmüller, Ralf. *Papermaking: The Art and Craft of Handmade Paper*. San Diego: Thorfinn International Marketing Consultants Inc. 1984. 62 pages. Originally written in German and translated into English. Content includes the history of papermaking, pulp preparation, additives, sheetforming, pressing, drying, making envelopes, watermarks, building a mould and deckle and a press, and a description and diagram of modern papermaking. Appropriate for middle school and older.

Collage

Brommer, Gerald F. *The Art of Collage.* Worcester, Massachusetts: Davis Publications, Inc. 1978. 176 pages. Paper is the element most commonly used in the art of collage. This book is full of pictures, ideas, and techniques. Appropriate selected chapters are "Paper Collage and Drawing," "Paper Collage and Painting," "Paper Collage and Printmaking," and "Introducing Other Materials."

Printmaking

Ayres, Julia. *Monotype: Mediums and Methods for Painterly Printmaking.* New York: Watson–Guptill Publications. 144 pages. Well–illustrated with many color photographs of printmakers' work. Content includes materials, basic techniques, methods of transfer, water–based and oil–based mediums, masks, stencils, embossment and collage, monoprints, and supply sources.

Decorated Papers

Chambers, Anne. *A Guide to Making Decorated Papers.* New York: Thames and Hudson Inc. 1989. 79 pages. Instructions for paste papers, block–printed papers, orizomegami, resist batik, stencil papers, oil marbling and suminagashi.

Guyot, Don. *Suminagashi.* Seattle: Brass Galley Press. 1988. 20 pages. A concise, clear guide to the art of suminagashi marbling.

Maurer, Diane Vogel. *Marbling.* New York: Crescent Books. 1991. 120 pages. Beautiful color photographs of marbling. Topics include suminagashi, watercolor and oil–color marbling, constructing marbling equipment and a paper project section. An excellent book for beginners.

Maurer–Mathison, Diane V. *Decorative Paper.* New York: Michael Friedman Publishing Group, Inc. 1993. 120 pages. Many color photographs of decorative paper. Covers paste papers, direct printing, orizomegami, batik, stencil prints, paper cutting, embossing, suminagashi, oil color marbling and paper projects.

Taylor, Carol. *Marbling Paper & Fabric.* New York: Sterling Publishing Co., Inc. 1991. 128 pages. Well–written instructions for learning the art of marbling. Lots of color photographs and helpful diagrams. Includes a project section.

Paper Projects And Paper Craft

A'Court, Angela and Marion Elliot. *Papercrafts.* London: Anness Publishing Limited. 1993. 128 pages. Describes over 100 paper projects, with 400 color photographs. Projects include oriental fans, envelopes, boxes, bags, decorative papers, quilling, pop–up cards, books, and jewelry.

Chatani, Masahiro. *Origamic Architecture.* Japan: Ondorisha Publishers. 1984. 87 pages. Presents the basics for making pop–up cards, as well as a variety of specific architectural plans. For all ages.

Ekiguchi, Kunio. *Gift Wrapping: Creative Ideas from Japan.* New York: Kodansha International Ltd. 1985. 124 pages. 66 different ways to beautifully wrap presents.

Jackson, Paul. *The Encyclopedia of Origami and Papercraft Techniques.* Philadelphia: Running Press. 1991. 192 pages. Techniques include origami, pop–ups, paper sculpture, papier–mâché, papermaking, découpage, model making, paper engineering, paper cuts, quilling, packaging and weaving. Another section of the book includes beautifully photographed examples of paper artists' work. There is a great variety in the types of work shown and the quality of the work is top notch. Inspiring!

Jackson, Paul. *The Pop–Up Book.* New York: Henry Hold and Company. 1993. 160 pages. Techniques, projects and examples by professional pop–up artists. Beautifully illustrated with color photos.

Kitagawa, Yoshiko. *Creative Cards: Wrap a Message with a Personal Touch.* New York: Kodansha International Ltd. 1990. All sorts of intriguing ideas for cutting, folding, and decorating your own cards.

Newman, Jay Hartley, Lee Scott Newman and Thelma Newman. *Paper as Art and Craft: The Complete Book of the History and Process of the Paper Art.* New York: Crown Publishers, Inc. 1973. 308 pages. A very comprehensive book. Chapters are "Paper: History and Process" (hand and machine papermaking, types of papers); "A Paper Vocabulary" (various paper manipulations, such as pleating, twisting and scoring); "Paper in Two Dimensions" (printmaking, rubbings, weaving, cutouts, mosaics); "Paper in Relief" (containers, origami, kites); "Sculptural and Architectural Forms;" "Collage, Découpage and Papier–Mâché;" "Decorative Papers and Bookbinding;" and "Useful and Decorative Forms" (paper beads, quilling, boxes and lampshades).

Pelham, David. *The Penguin Book of Kites*. New York: Penguin Books. 1976. 227 pages. A very comprehensive book about kites. Includes history, construction, flying and a variety of kite patterns.

Shannon, Faith. *Paper Pleasures*. New York: Weidenfeld & Nicolson. 1987. 168 pages. Offers instructions for making paper, for decorating papers with different printing methods. Shows different objects that can be made using paper, such as boxes, jewelry, books, frames and many other items. Although the technical information is incomplete, the beautiful color photographs are very inspiring.

Book Arts

Ikegami, Kojiro. *Japanese Bookbinding*. New York: Weatherhill. 1986. 127 pages. Describes in great detail a variety of Japanese bookbinding techniques.

Johnson, Pauline. *Creative Bookbinding*. Seattle: University of Washington Press. 1977. The contents include book design, the parts of a book, materials and tools, simple constructions and binding procedures, decorated papers and supply sources. Also offers suggestions for working with children.

Smith, Keith. *Non–Adhesive Binding*. Rochester, New York: keith smith BOOKS. 1991. 318 pages. Detailed instructions for 32 simple bindings, accompanied by 250 drawings. Probably most appropriate for high school and above.

Calligraphy

Charatan, Karen. *ABC ZIG Calligraphy*. New Jersey: EK Success. 1993. 44 pages. Includes instructions and many colorful, creative examples of calligraphy using ZIG markers.

Papercutting

Christensen, J.A. *Cut–Art: An Introduction to Chung–Hua and Kiri–E*. New York: Watson–Guptill Publications. 1989. Step by step instruction, beginning with the very simplest through more advanced projects. This is the Japanese version of papercutting. Many different cultures foster the art of papercutting, each one maintaining their own distinctive techniques.

Rich, Chris. *The Book of Paper Cutting: A Complete Guide to All the Techniques.* New York: Sterling Publishing Company, Inc. 1993. 128 pages. This book covers several different cultures' techniques. Although most projects are very complex, there are several simple enough to be adapted for the classroom.

Photography

Reeve, Catharine and Marilyn Sward. *The New Photography*. Englewood Cliffs, New Jersey: Prentice–Hall, Inc. 1983. 241 pages. An excellent guide to all non–silver photography. Includes making paper and using it for photography.

Pulp Painting

Hockney, David. *Paper Pools*. New York: Harry N. Abrams. 1980. 100 pages. Examples of pulp painting, with lots of photographs and illustrations. The text shows how one artist develops his ideas.

Sculpture

Williams, Arthur. *Sculpture: Technique–Form–Content.* Worcester, Massachusetts: Davis Publications. 1990. 368 pages, 800 photos. Although this book is about sculpture in general, an entire chapter is devoted to using paper pulp, including casting technique and building up over armatures. Other useful chapters include mouldmaking, careers in sculpture, and mixed media.

MOVIES and VIDEOS

Barrett, Timothy. *Papermaking*. Iowa City, Iowa: University of Iowa Center for the Book. 1994. A series of five videos for teachers, students, artists, and anyone with interests in the history and technique of Western and Japanese papermaking. Three tapes (80 minutes, 37 minutes, and 39 minutes) deal with simple, traditional and professional Japanese papermaking. Two tapes (30 minutes, 27 minutes) cover classroom and professional equipment and techniques for Western papermaking. Package includes a tape transcript, a bibliography, and a list of papermaking suppliers.

Berman, Aaron. *Paper and Gold*. Boston: Berman Video Production. 1994. 15 minutes. Shows the incredible process of how bamboo paper is made for use in gold–beating (gold–leaf) in Burma.

Clark, Howard and Kathryn. *The Mark of the Maker*. Chicago: McGowan Film and Video. 1990. 27 minutes. Available in VHS videocassette or 16mm film. Inspirational as well as instructional. Demonstrates not only how paper is made by hand, but why people make paper by hand.

Gallo, Frank. *Hand Papermaking Video Series*. Urbana, Illinois: The Pulpers. 1992. Five videos, each running 5 to 10 minutes. Titles are: "Sheet Forming and Pulp Preparation," "Hand Papermaking as an Art Medium," "Sculptural Papermaking," "Paper Casting and Mold Making," "Artist Profile: Frank Gallo."

Grummer, Arnold. *Papermaking for Everyone*. Appleton, WI: Greg Markim, Inc. 198–. 57 minute video. Shows how to make paper with the pour hand mold, recycling, more.

Hand Papermaking. *Hand Papermaking Video*. Washington, D.C.: Hand Papermaking. 1992. Features work and commentary of 30 artists working in the medium of handmade paper. High school level.

Koretsky, Elaine. *The Last Papermakers on the Silk Road*. Brookline, MA: Carriage House. 1993. 18 minutes. Documents "old" papermaking still being practiced in China.

National Geographic Video. *Living Treasures of Japan*. Stamford, Connecticut: Vestron Video. 1980. One featured "living treasures" is Ashiro Abe, a papermaker. The segment shows him making paper in his village.

Recycle It Yourself. Chicago, IL: Jack Schmidling. 1990.

Strathmore Paper Company. *Paper Is Part Of The Picture*. Boston, MA: Cinema Graphics/Video One. 1987.

Traditional Crafts of Japan. New Canaan, CT: Diamond, Inc. 1992. Includes sections about weaving, dyeing, ceramics, lacquer, woodworking, metal-working, brushes and sumi ink, as well as a 25–minute segment on paper-making in the Echizen Region of Northern Japan.

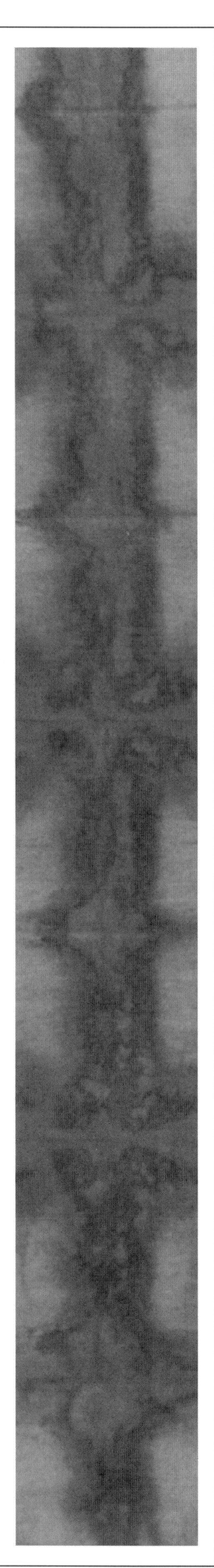

Appendix

Teachers are busy people, so I've included some materials which can be photocopied to use in the classroom. I hope this makes your life easier and your teaching more effective.

HOW TO MAKE YOUR OWN PAPER AT HOME

(short version)

CAUTION: ALWAYS ASK AN ADULT FOR PERMISSION TO DO THIS ACTIVITY!!!!!!!

1. Gather paper to recycle into pulp.
2. Soak the paper and tear it into little pieces.
3. (*Optional*) Put the paper in a pot, cover it completely with water, and cook for one hour.
4. If the paper has been cooked, let it cool; put a small handful in the blender with four cups of water and blend until the paper becomes pulp.
5. Put the pulp in a vat and add water if the pulp is too thick.
6. Form a sheet by scooping up the pulp with a mould (either aluminum window screen with duct tape on the edges, or an embroidery hoop with fiberglass window screen).
7. Turn the mould over onto your felt (any kind of fabric will do), press on the back of the screen and then, remove the mould.
8. Press the paper with a sponge or rolling pin, or use a board with a heavy weight on top.
9. Leave the paper on the fabric to dry. Remove the sheet of paper when it is dry. To flatten the paper, put it under some heavy books.

Have fun and remember there are lots of books on papermaking at your library!

HOW TO MAKE YOUR OWN PAPER AT HOME

(short version)

CAUTION: ALWAYS ASK AN ADULT FOR PERMISSION TO DO THIS ACTIVITY!!!!!!!

1. Gather paper to recycle into pulp.
2. Soak the paper and tear it into little pieces.
3. (*Optional*) Put the paper in a pot, cover it completely with water, and cook for one hour.
4. If the paper has been cooked, let it cool; put a small handful in the blender with four cups of water and blend until the paper becomes pulp.
5. Put the pulp in a vat and add water if the pulp is too thick.
6. Form a sheet by scooping up the pulp with a mould (either aluminum window screen with duct tape on the edges, or an embroidery hoop with fiberglass window screen).
7. Turn the mould over onto your felt (any kind of fabric will do), press on the back of the screen and then, remove the mould.
8. Press the paper with a sponge or rolling pin, or use a board with a heavy weight on top.
9. Leave the paper on the fabric to dry. Remove the sheet of paper when it is dry. To flatten the paper, put it under some heavy books.

Have fun and remember there are lots of books on papermaking at your library!

HOW TO MAKE YOUR OWN PAPER AT HOME (detailed version)

CAUTION: ALWAYS ASK AN ADULT FOR PERMISSION TO DO THIS ACTIVITY!!!!!!!!!!

Basic Supplies:

Blender (find at garage sales or thrift stores for $3 – $5, if you don't already have one)
Window screen — either fiberglass (soft) or aluminum (stiff)
Duct tape
Vat (dishpan or other container for pulp)
Stainless steel or enameled pot for cooking pulp
Coloring — food color, tempera paint, acrylic paint, watercolors, etc.
(If it dissolves in water, it will work, although some types work better than others.)
Felts (Wool felt is traditionally used, but almost any fabric such as towels or sheets will do.)
Newspapers — helps eliminate water spills on the floor
Paper for recycling into pulp

Optional Supplies:

Embroidery hoop
Cookie cutters

STEP ONE: Making moulds

Moulds can be made in many ways. Two very simple versions are described below.

Small screen moulds • Cut a piece of aluminum screen about one inch larger than the size of the paper you plan to make, but no larger than six inches square, or the mould will be too awkward to handle. Cover the edges of the screen with duct tape by placing the middle of the tape at the edge of the screen and pressing the tape around both sides of the screen. Other moulds may be created by cutting screens in a variety of shapes for use in laminating images on paper.

Embroidery hoop moulds • Choose an embroidery hoop the same size that you want the mould. (Plastic hoops stand up best to the constant moisture of papermaking.) Cut a piece of fiberglass window screen about an inch larger than the plastic hoop. Stretch the screen over the hoop, secure it as you would with fabric and you're ready to roll.

STEP TWO: Making felts

Cut the fabric at least four inches larger than the size of paper you plan to make.

STEP THREE: Making pulp by recycling paper

1. Gather paper to recycle into pulp. Colored paper, such as construction paper, can be divided into separate colors, eliminating the need to color the pulp later. When choosing paper to recycle, remember that the quality of the recycled paper determines the quality of the finished paper. Starting with newspaper means the final paper will have the quality of newsprint. Avoid shiny papers and other papers, such as coffee filters which are designed to not break down when wet.
2. Soak the papers overnight.
3. Tear the paper into approximately one–inch squares.
4. (Optional) Place in a cooking pot and cover the paper with water. Place the pot on the stove and bring the water to a boil. Cover the pot and cook the paper for one hour.

5. After cooking, remove it from the stove and let the paper cool. After cooled, the paper may be processed immediately.
6. To process the paper into pulp, put 4 cups of water in a blender.
7. Add a small handful of the cooked paper.

CAUTION: DO NOT ADD TOO MUCH PAPER AT ONE TIME. IF YOU DO, THE PAPER WILL NOT BE ADEQUATELY BEATEN AND THERE IS DANGER OF BURNING UP THE BLENDER MOTOR.

8. Turn on the blender to its highest speed and leave it on until the paper is thoroughly broken down.
9. Add color, if desired. Color may be added to small amounts of pulp while blending or, after making a large quantity, color it all at once in a bucket.
10. To store the pulp until use, drain the water and put in plastic bags. Pulp usually keeps in the refrigerator for about two weeks. In the freezer, pulp keeps indefinitely. Remember, pulp comes from a plant and, over time, it does the same thing fruits and vegetables do. The smell will tell you if you have kept the pulp too long!

STEP FOUR: Sheetforming

1. Fill a vat half full of water.
2. Add the pulp to the vat. Using more pulp creates thicker paper. (Through experience, you will eventually know how much pulp to add for the desired thickness of paper.)
3. Dip one of your newly made moulds into the vat and scoop up pulp to form a sheet.
4. Turn the mould over onto the felt so the pulp is touching the felt.
5. Using a sponge, press on the back of the screen to remove some of the water and make the fibers stick to the felt.
6. Lift the mould, starting at one edge and gently "rolling" it up, leaving the fibers on the felt.

STEP FIVE: Pressing the sheet

Sheets may be pressed in many ways.

- Place another felt on top of your sheet and roll a rolling pin over the felt.
- Place a fiberglass screen over the top of your sheet and press with a sponge.
- Place another felt on top of the paper. Put a board on the felt and add a heavy weight on top of the board.

STEP SIX: Drying the paper

Paper may be dried in a number of ways.

- Leave the paper on the felt, lay it on a flat surface or hang on a clothesline and let it air dry. When it is completely dry, peel the paper away from the felt.
- Lay the handmade paper between absorbent papers, such as newspaper or blotter paper, and put a few books on top. Place in front of a fan to dry. Speed up the process by exchanging wet absorbent paper for dry absorbent paper every two hours.

Remember, there are lots of good books in your library to teach you even more about paper-making. Good luck and have a good time!

WORLD Map

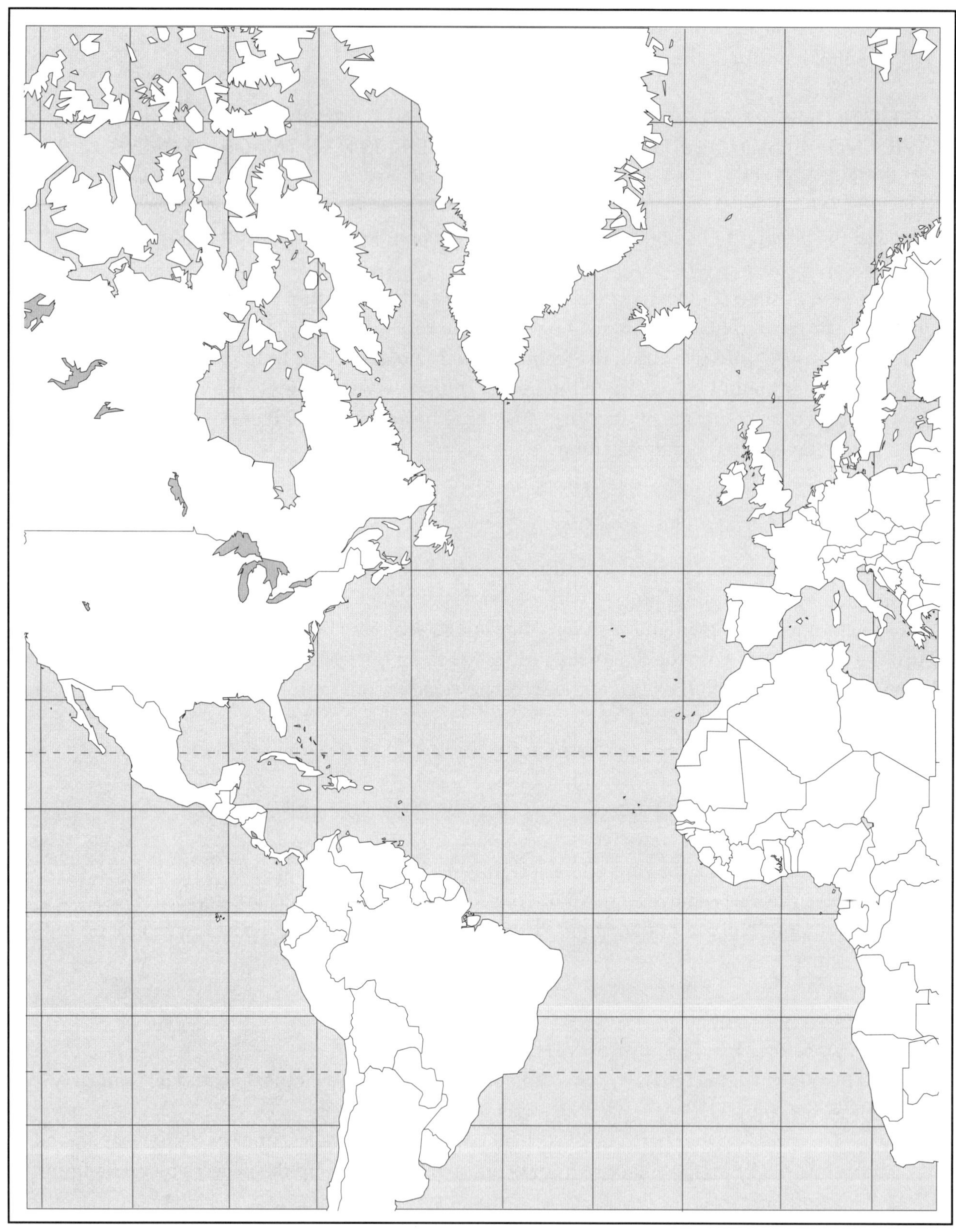

WORLD Map

UNITED STATES Map

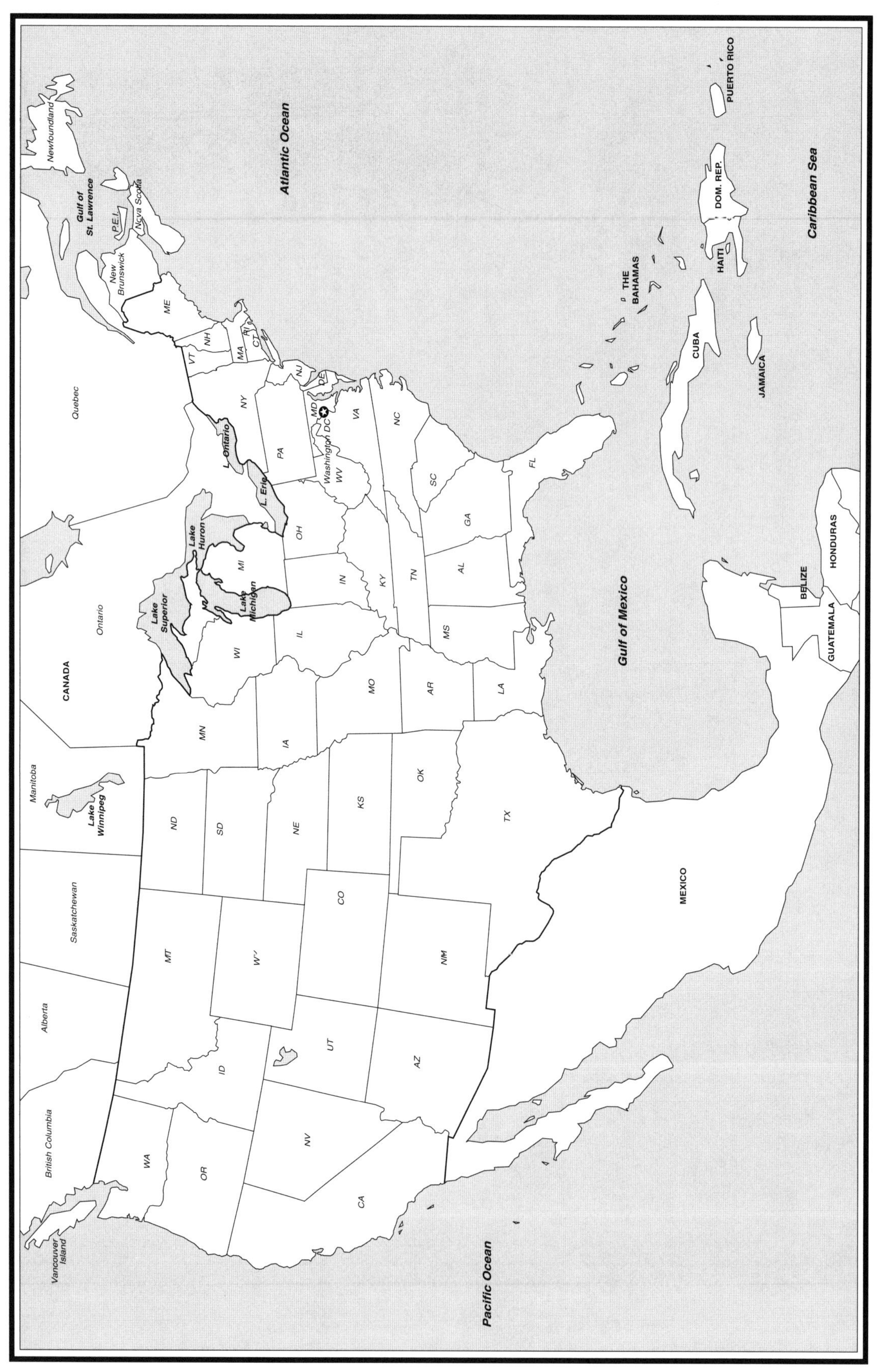

SEQUENCING

gather fiber	soak fiber
cook fiber	beat fiber
color fiber (optional)	form sheets using a mould and deckle
couch the paper onto a felt (turn over the mould with the fibers on it onto the fabric)	press the paper
dry the paper	admire the results

1. Cut two squares of paper. One square must be 1/4–inch larger than the other. ACCURACY IS IMPORTANT!

2. Starting at opposite corners of the paper, mark diagonal lines with a pencil.

3. Fold corners to the center "X".

4. Fold two opposite sides to the center point. Unfold.

5. Fold the other two opposite sides to the center. Unfold.

6. Cut on the fold lines on two opposite edges. You will have two cuts on opposite edges (4 total cuts).

7. On the sides where you have cut, pull out the two opposite sides. Fold up the sides that have not been pulled out to form a box.

8. Bring the pulled–out side over the folded–up sides and glue down on the inside, if necessary.

9. Repeat steps 2 through 8 for the other square.

10. If folded accurately, the larger square will fit neatly over the smaller square to form a wonderful covered box!

Directions for MAKING ORIGAMI BOXES

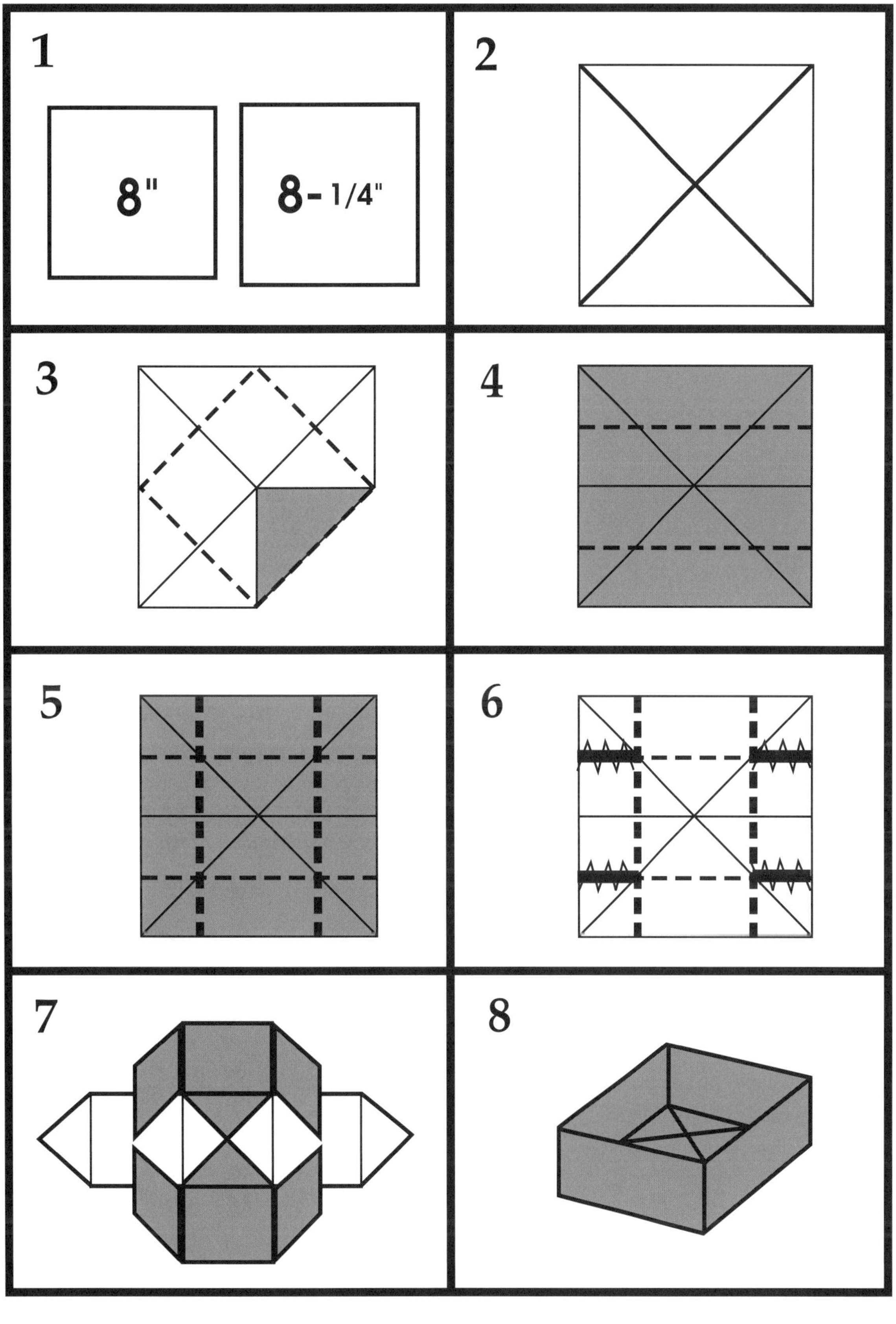

1

8"

8-1/4"

2

3

4

5

6

7

8

1) Neatly pile the sheets of your text in a stack.
2) Place one cover sheet on top and one cover sheet on the bottom. The cover is often slightly larger and chosen from a heavier weight paper than the paper which is used for the text. If you are using the same weight of paper for the cover as for the text, make it heavier by using a sheet which is twice as big and folding it in half, with the fold being the outer edge and opposite the side where you bind.
3) Use a pencil to lightly mark the cover with the locations where holes are to be punched. Four is a traditional number of holes, but any number will work.
4) Position the pages between the two covers. Keep the pages from shifting by placing several clothespins along the edge of the book to be bound.
5) Punch the holes in the binding with an awl, ice pick or similar tool.
6) Select a thread and a needle for sewing your book. In Japan, silk and hemp are traditionally used. I often use a readily available cotton warp thread, but try any thread you have on hand. For decorative purposes, you can use more than one thread.
7) Begin to sew by starting at any hole on the spine of the book. Lift two or three sheets of the text. Insert the needle under these sheets and bring it up through the hole and out, leaving a short tail inside the book. Bring the needle around the spine to the front of the book and then up again through the same hole. Proceed to the next hole and continue, as shown in the drawings.
8) Continue stitching until you eventually return to the place where you started. Put the needle back through the same hole and bring it out between the two sheets of text where you began. Tie the thread with its tail and snip off the threads at the knot.

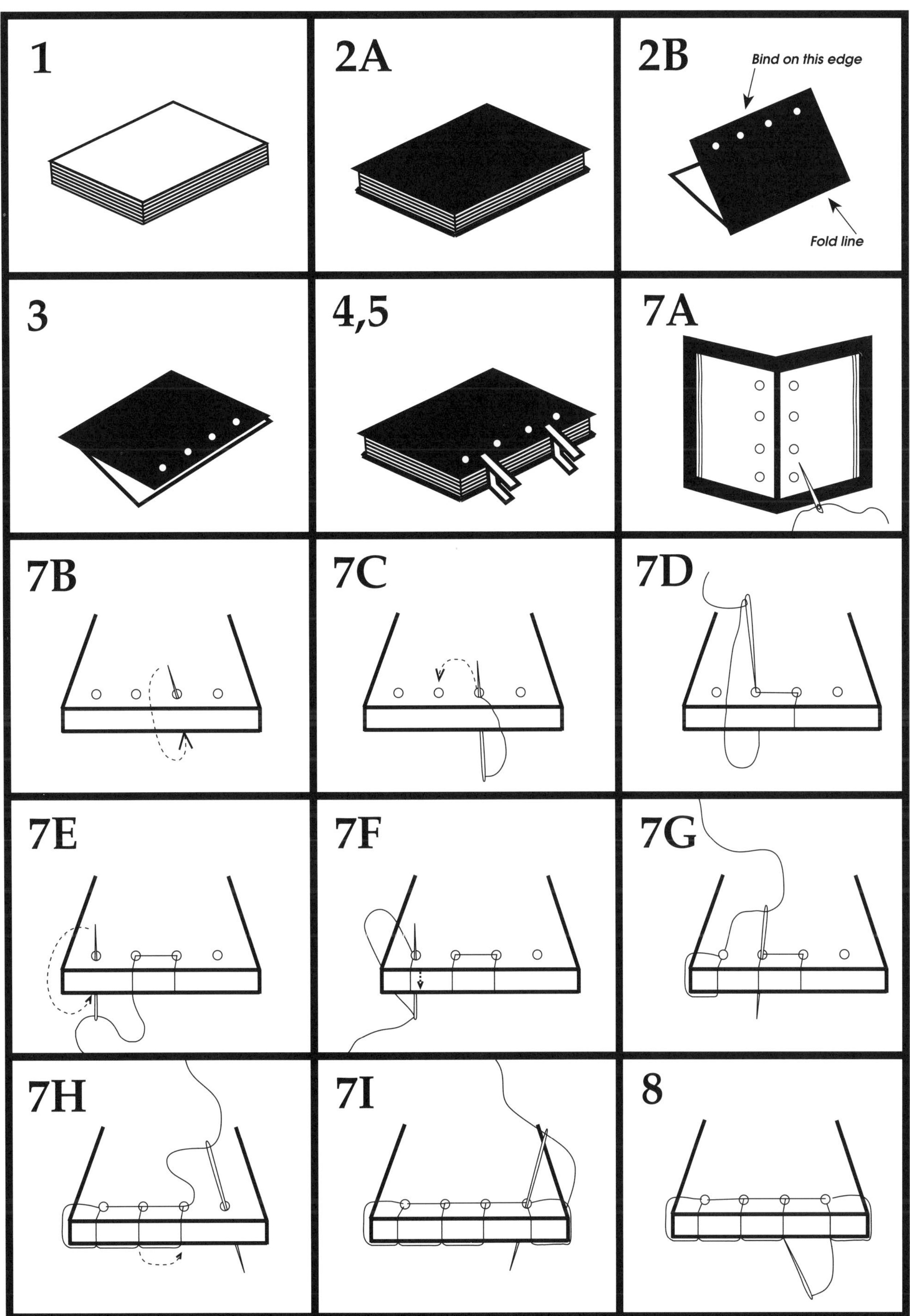
1
2A
2B
Bind on this edge
Fold line
3
4,5
7A
7B
7C
7D
7E
7F
7G
7H
7I
8

Diagrams for THE SCIENCE OF PAPERMAKING by Timothy Barrett

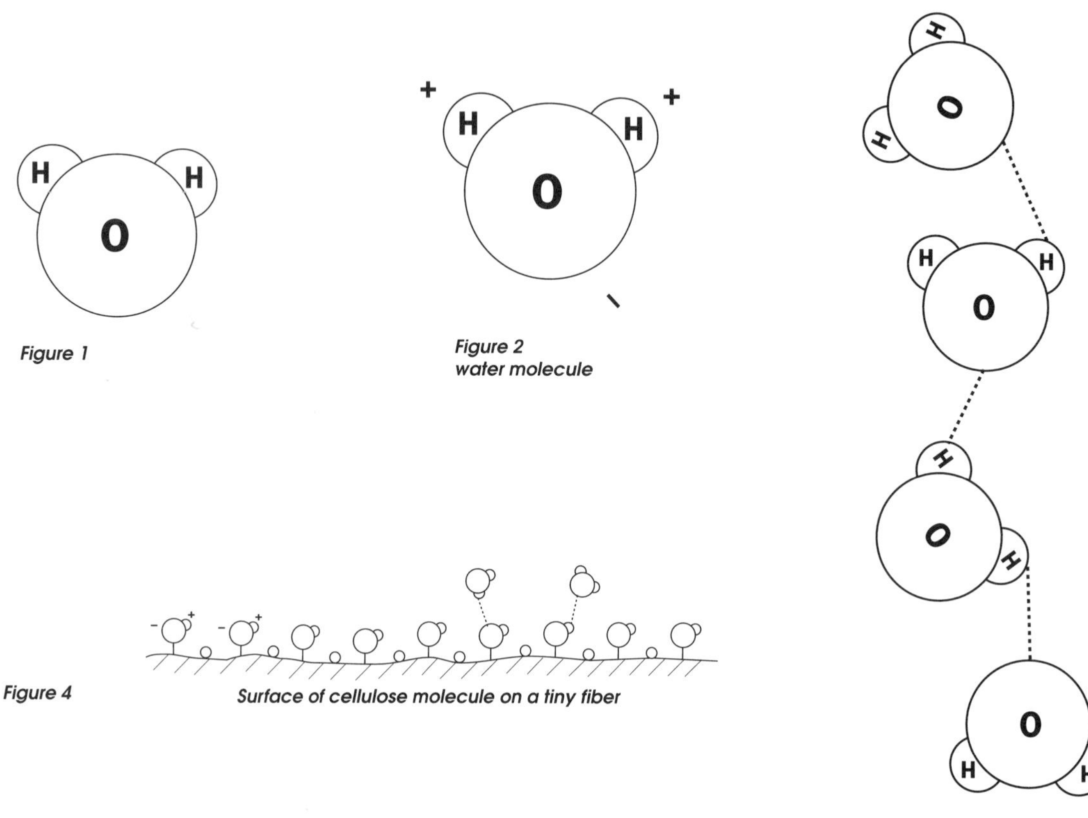

Figure 1

Figure 2
water molecule

Figure 3
hydrogen bond

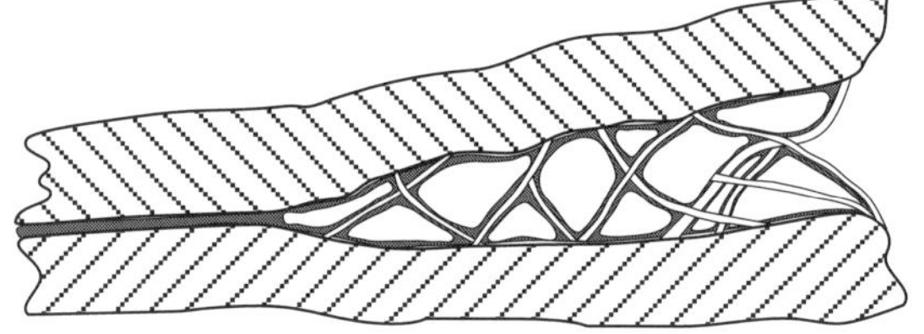

Figure 4 **Surface of cellulose molecule on a tiny fiber**

Figure 5
fibrils on cellulose surfaces during water removal

Source: James D'A. Clark. *Pulp Technology and Treatment for Paper*. Miller Freeman. 1978.

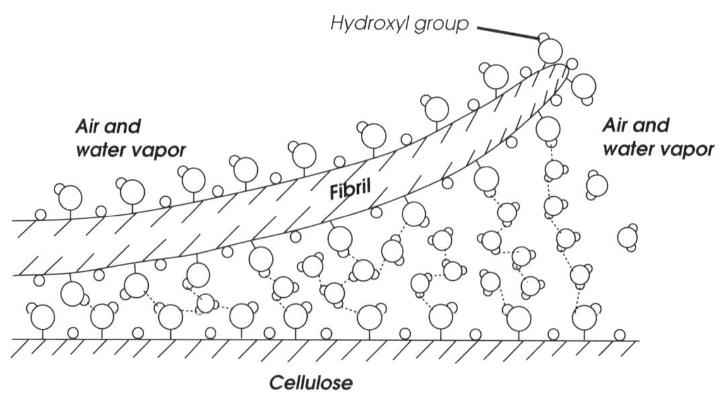

Figure 6
water molecules between two cellulose surfaces

Source: James D'A. Clark. *Pulp Technology and Treatment for Paper*. Miller Freeman. 1978.

SUPPLIERS AND OTHER USEFUL RESOURCES

Papermaking Suppliers

Free catalogues are available from all the following papermaking suppliers. Catalogues provide lots of information about how to use the products. As a beginning papermaker, I learned a lot just by reading catalogues.

Twinrocker Papermaking Supplies
P.O. Box 413
Brookston, IN 47923
317–563–3119 or 1–800–757–TWIN

Carriage House Papermaking Supplies
P.O. Box 197
North Hatfield, MA 01066
Tel/Fax: 413 / 247–5668

Dieu Donné Papermill Inc.
433 Broome Street
New York, NY 10013–2622
Phone: 212 / 226–0573
FAX: 212 / 226–6088

The Papertrail
1546 Chatelain Avenue
Ottawa, Ontario, Canada K1Z 8B5
Phone: 613 / 728–4669
FAX: 613 / 728–7796

Lee Scott McDonald, Inc.
P.O. Box 264
Charlestown, MA 02129
Phone: 617 / 242–2505 FAX: 617 / 242–8825

Magnolia Papermaking Supplies
2527 Magnolia Street
Oakland, CA 94607
Phone: 510 / 839–5268 FAX: 510 / 893–8834

Gold's Artwork, Inc.
2100 North Pine Street
Lumberton, NC 28358
Phone: 1–800–356–2306

Kakali Handmade Papers
1249 Cartwright Street, Granville Island
Vancouver, B.C., Canada V6A 3R7
Phone: 604 / 682–5274

School Suppliers who carry Papermaking Supplies

Dick Blick
P.O. Box 1267
Galesburg, IL 61402–1267
1–800–723–2787

Triarco Arts and Crafts
14650 – 28th Avenue North
Plymouth, MN 55441
1–800–328–3360

Pyramid
Box 877
Urbana, IL 61801
1–800–252–1363

Sax Arts and Craft
P.O. Box 51710
New Berlin, WI 53151
1–800–558–6696

NASCO
901 Janesville Avenue, Box 901
Fort Atkinson, WI 53538–0901
1–800–558–9595

J. L. Hammett Co.
1 Hammett Place
Braintree, MA 02184
1–800–333–4600

Sources for Beaten Pulp in Your Area

Zpapersmith
384 – 21st Street SE, P.O. Box 1294
Cedar Rapids, IA 52403–1294
Phone or FAX: 319 / 365–9611

Columbia College Chicago
Center for the Book and Paper Arts
218 S. Wabash
Chicago, IL 60604–2316
Phone: 312 / 431–8612

Paper Arts Mill and Studio
Box 60203
Phoenix, AZ 85082
Phone: 602 / 966–1998

Cave Paper
1334 – 6th Street NE
Minneapolis, MN 55413
Phone: 612 / 378–2696

Seapen Press and Paper Mill
2228 NE 46th Street
Seattle, WA 98105
Phone: 206 / 522–3879

Other Useful Resources

American Museum of Papermaking
Institute of Paper Science and Technology
500 10th Street, NW
Atlanta, Georgia 30318–5794 Telephone: 404 / 853–9590

This museum houses the Dard Hunter collection. Its exhibitions are to designed to preserve the cultural and technological contributions that paper has made to past and present civilizations and to project future technologies of papermaking.

Hand Papermaking Magazine
P.O. Box 77027
Washington D.C. 20013–7027

This professional journal covers a wide range of papermaking activities from around the world, and includes a paper sample in each issue. Write for subscription information and availability of back issues.

The Friends of Dard Hunter
N8279 Island View Road
Fish Creek, WI 54212–9734

Inspired by the life, writings, and museum collection of Dard Hunter (1883-1966), the Friends of Dard Hunter is an organization which serves all those for whom paper is something special, bringing together the wide range of artistic, craft, archival, historic, printing, book arts, educational, and scientific interests which paper can inspire. Through its newsletter and other publications, at its conferences, and by the networking potential of its membership Directory, the Friends of Dard Hunter offers knowledge, expertise, and most importantly, national, and international friendship, connections and opportunities associated with a common and passionate interest in paper. Write for membership information.

Minnesota Center for the Book Arts
24 North Third Street
Minneapolis, MN 55401

This center is an exhibition, education and production facility dedicated to preserving and promoting the book arts, which includes papermaking. Programs and services offer classes for children and adults. A school tours program, with hands–on activities for children in grades K–8, is also available.

Columbia College Chicago
Center for the Book and Paper Arts
218 S. Wabash, 7th Floor
Chicago, IL 60604–2316
312 / 431–8612

Offers classes for the community, as well as graduate and undergraduate credit.

Historic Rittenhouse Town
206 Lincoln Drive
Philadelphia, PA 19144
215 / 438–5711 Visitor Center
215 / 843–2228 Paper Studio

Historic Rittenhouse Town, now part of Fairmount Park in Philadelphia, PA, was the site of the first papermill in the North American colonies. William Rittenhouse arrived here from Holland in 1688, and by 1690, was manufacturing fine white paper. Rittenhouse Town remained the center of papermaking in American for nearly 100 years.

Today, this National Historic Landmark is dedicated to teaching the tradition of hand papermaking. Classes are offered year round for children, adults, artists, teachers, and families. Through advance registration, special guided tours are available for groups, and the Visitor Center is open to the public most weekends throughout the year. For information, call the Visitor Center or Paper Studio.

Lockwood–Post's Directory
San Francisco: Miller Freeman Publications.

Addresses of most any company in, or allied to, the commercial paper industry can be found in this annual directory. Many of the large companies have public relations departments that can provide books, posters, videos and other educational materials, developed for schools, which are free for the asking.

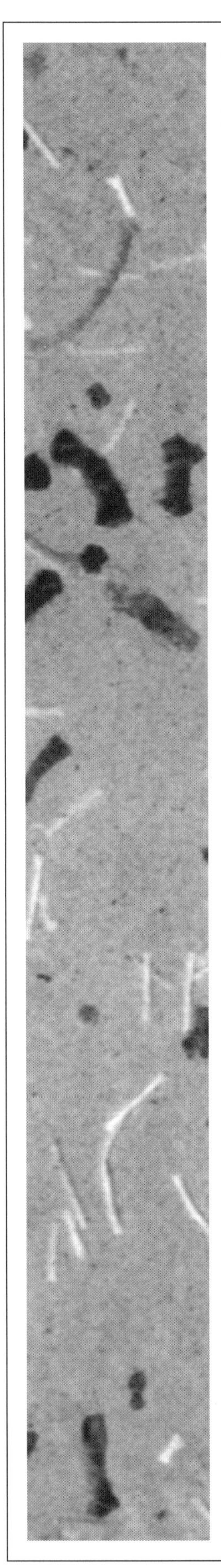

Index

A

B

C

D

I

J

K

L

M

N

O

P

Q

R

S

T

U

V

W

Z

ABOUT THE AUTHOR

Gloria Zmolek Smith is a public school art teacher turned paper artist. She has studied with many of the most knowledgeable papermakers in the country and has been successfully exhibiting her works nationally for the past ten years. Zmolek Smith also teaches papermaking classes for adults, educators and children in schools across Iowa and surrounding states. She lives in Cedar Rapids, Iowa with her husband Tom, son Nathan, daughter Laurel, dog Pooky, and hamster Sparkie.

Timothy Barrett is an associate research scientist at the University of Iowa Center for the Book (UICB). His duties include teaching papermaking history and techniques at the School of Art and Art History, and overseeing research and production at the separate UICB facility.

COLOPHON

Teaching Hand Papermaking: A Classroom Guide was written on an Apple IIgs with one 3.5″ 800K floppy drive and 1.2 MB RAM, using AppleWorks 3.0 for word processing of original drafts. Text was saved in ASCII format for file translation. Drafts were printed on an Apple ImageWriter dot–matrix printer.

Some file translation was done on a Macintosh SE/30, with System 6.0.7, System 6.0.8 and Apple File Exchange.

Additional file translation, editing, illustrations (except those for the read–aloud history of papermaking), typesetting, page layout and positioning of 139 halftones and 62 illustrations was done on a Macintosh Centris 650/80MB, with 24 MB RAM and the following software applications:

Macintosh System 7.1	Aldus PageMaker 4.2a and 5.0
Apple File Exchange 7.0	Aldus FreeHand 3.11
WordPerfect 1.0.5 and 3.0	Adobe TypeManager 3.6
Cartesia MapArt, Vol. 1	

Files were stored on a Cutting Edge 80MB external hard drive and a MicroNet Advantage 88MB C SyQuest® Removable Hard Disk Cartridge drive, using ten 88MB cartridges.

Typefaces are Adobe Palatino for headings and body text, and Adobe Avant Garde for captions.

Halftones were scanned on an AppleOne Scanner (grayscale at 300 dpi), using a PowerMacintosh 8100/80, with 40 MB RAM and a 1GB hard drive; a Macintosh IIcx, with 8MB RAM and a 1GB hard drive. Software applications used were Macintosh System 7.5, Adobe Photoshop 2.5.1 and Light Source Ofoto 2.0.1.

Proofs and final prints were made on a Xanté AccelaWriter 8100 PostScript 600dpi laser printer on 24 lb. Hammermill Laser Print bond paper. Final output is to a Linotronic 530 imagesetter.

Final offset printing of the document body is on acid–free 60 lb. Finch Opaque Smooth book paper. The cover is 10 pt. C1S cover stock, with film lamination. Offset printing and perfect binding were done at Thomson–Shore, Dexter, Michigan.

Graphic design and production is by Jill J. Jensen, Jensen Management/Communications, Cedar Rapids, Iowa.

If you would like to order a signed copy of

Teaching Hand Papermaking: A Classroom Guide

by Gloria Zmolek Smith

Make a *check* payable to Zpaperpress for $27.45 ($24.95 plus $2.50 shipping) for each book ordered. Iowa residents should add $1.25 sales tax per book. Send the check to:

Zpaperpress
384 – 21st Street SE
P.O. Box 1294
Cedar Rapids, IA 52406–1294

For *Mastercard* or *VISA* orders, send your name, credit card number, expiration date, and your signature, with the number of books desired, to the above address. For faster service, you may phone or fax this information to 319 / 365–9611.

Quantity orders invited. For bulk discount prices please call 319 / 365–9611.